MANUAL OF BUSINESS LIBRARY PRACTICE

MANUAL OF
BUSINESS LIBRARY
PRACTICE

edited by

Malcolm J Campbell

CLIVE BINGLEY
LONDON

LINNET BOOKS
HAMDEN · CONN

FIRST PUBLISHED 1975 BY CLIVE BINGLEY LTD
16 PEMBRIDGE ROAD LONDON W11
SIMULTANEOUSLY PUBLISHED IN THE USA BY LINNET BOOKS
AN IMPRINT OF THE SHOE STRING PRESS INC
995 SHERMAN AVENUE HAMDEN CONNECTICUT 06514
SET IN 10 ON 12 POINT TIMES ROMAN
PHOTOSET, PRINTED AND BOUND IN GREAT BRITAIN BY
REDWOOD BURN LTD TROWBRIDGE AND ESHER
COPYRIGHT © MALCOLM J CAMPBELL 1975

CLIVE BINGLEY ISBN: 0–85157–178–8
LINNET BOOKS ISBN: 0–208–01359–8

Z
675
B8
M30

Library of Congress Cataloging in Publication Data

Main entry under title:

Manual of business library practice.

Bibliography: p.
1. Business libraries.   2. Business—Information services.
I. Campbell, Malcolm J.
Z675.B8M35   1975   027.6'9   75–20223
ISBN 0–208–01359–8

Contents

5

Introduction

Business (or commercial) librarians have for long questioned whether there has been adequate education for their particular branch of librarianship, even allowing for the fact that there is much that can be learned only through on-the-job training. Some library schools do run well planned courses for students choosing this option, but lecturers must have difficulty in describing materials which may be held by only a few public reference libraries in the UK. It is a field of rapidly changing developments, opening up or closing off whole areas of information provision. In the period of a few recent months for instance, the principal source of data on newly registered United Kingdom companies ceased publication in a manageable form, one of London's largest collections of trade journals has closed its doors to the public at large, but new and expensive services describing major companies and industry sectors in detail have proliferated.

So business librarianship is not the easiest of disciplines for either the student or lecturer to master. But ill equipped practitioners can do little to improve a situation in which, in the case of local authorities at least, services to the business community seem generally to have a low priority in what regrettably is still regarded as a 'welfare' service. A strong corps of enthusiastic professionals is needed to combat this attitude.

To some degree the unsatisfactory state of preparation of students for work in business or commercial libraries must be due to the lack of texts on the subject. This book is an attempt partially to fill this gap. It opens with a consideration of how the structure of business information provision in this country has evolved and the relationship of the component parts to each other, particularly through the development of schemes for interlibrary cooperation. There follows a section on the organisation and administration of business libraries, including planning, staffing, classification and cataloguing. Though written largely with the public library in mind, many of the principles may be adapted to the private sector, and a short contribution on the functions and workings of company business libraries is appended.

Some of the problems of acquisition and use of materials encountered are next dealt with—directories and company information sources, statistics and market research data, management books, newspapers, periodicals etc. Then there is a chapter on the exploitation of these materials by such means as book lists, library bulletins and 'current awareness' services.

The final section is devoted to an examination of a number of relevant external sources of information, recognising that no unit can operate in a vacuum, but will benefit from a consciousness of what is available elsewhere and under what conditions of accessibility. It will be seen that the *Manual* is by no means exhaustive; whole areas are not broached here, such as business law and the tracing of trade names. It was felt that the *Manual* should initially be kept to manageable proportions, leaving room for extension in any future edition to take account of users' reactions.

All the contributors write from experience of matters they deal with in their day to day work as—with one exception—practising librarians. The exception is George Henderson, who has turned from simply using business information sources to the creation of reference books hardly less essential to any library than *Whitaker's almanack* itself.

Some additional aspects of the subject are dealt with in my earlier *Business information services* (Bingley, 1974). This however was written largely with practitioners in mind, rather as one man's subjective and personal approach. There seemed to be room for a more formal treatment from a variety of pens, though they might cover some similar ground.

Finally I should express my thanks to the contributors, who allowed themselves to be persuaded to write for the *Manual* and patiently endured periodic bullying for copy, to Garry Humphreys of the City Business Library for encouragement and help, and to my wife, forbearing as ever in the face of extra-marital preoccupation.

November, 1974   MALCOLM J CAMPBELL

The contributors

Alan Armstrong was information officer at Kellogg International Corporation until leaving to devote full time to his own company. He contributed a regular column on industrial libraries to *New library world*.

David W Bromley FLA is Assistant Director, Reference and Information Services, at Sheffield, where he was previously the commercial librarian. Before this, he served at Nottingham and Coventry. Writings include *What to read on exporting* for the Library Association, now in its third edition. His co-author, Angela M Allott BA ALA, is currently in charge of commercial, scientific and technical information at Sheffield.

Malcolm J Campbell ALA joined the Corporation of London as City Business Librarian in 1968. He was employed by Holborn Public Libraries from 1946 to 1959, then was successively the librarian of the British Employers' Confederation and the Confederation of British Industry. Author of *Business information services* and, for Francis Hodgson, compiler of *Directory of financial directories*.

Frank Cochrane DGA FLA was the librarian of the Statistics and Market Intelligence Library, having started his career at Manchester Public Library, later moving to the Royal Military College of Science as deputy librarian. He is now Head of Technical Library Services, Department of Trade.

George P Henderson, Director of CBD Research Ltd, was with the Guildhall Library from 1938–1963, for much of that time being responsible for the Commercial Reference Room. After a period of time with Kelly's Directories, he established his own directory publishing house, the output of which includes *Current British directories*, companion volumes for Europe, Africa and (shortly) Asia, *European companies, Directory of British associations* and guides to statistical sources in Europe and the USA.

A Leslie Smyth FLA is Commercial Librarian and Information Officer at Manchester Central Library, which authority he has served since 1935. Has written a number of articles and a guide to the resources of his own library, which in itself constitutes an introduction to the subject of business information. MBE 1975.

Kenneth D C Vernon FLA Dip Lib has been the librarian of the London Graduate School of Business Studies since its inception in 1966. He has formerly been with the Royal Institute of British Architects, the Royal Society of Arts and the Royal Institution. With Valerie Lang was the compiler of the London Classification of Business Studies, now employed in a growing number of management libraries in the UK and elsewhere.

Chapter 1

The structure of commercial library information services

D W Bromley and A M Allott

Historical introduction

Commercial and business information is an inseparable part of the history of the developed industrial nations. In modern times, commercial data is flashed to all parts of the world via satellites, to be absorbed into the computerised information systems serving the major trading countries. What were the earliest manifestations of the need for similar information?

Early communities knew by oral tradition the needs of neighbouring communities. As soon as there was a surplus over production, or an unsatisfied need, they had to develop an early version of a market research report—who else had something to offer, what could be used to barter for it? Information (on trade, politics, religion, culture) flowed along the trade routes of the ancient world. Reliable information has always been a saleable commodity. Those who financed kings or countries had to be in a position where decision making was based on available information. Credit worthiness is the modern term for an evaluating process which all who lend or borrow have had to go through before acting on their decision. Once, a network of ambassadors fulfilled the functions of news gatherers and transmitters.

When power began to pass to any group of persons—noblemen, churchmen, merchants, corporations—then they too developed a need for accurate information. Shakespeare's 'What news on the Rialto?' is a forerunner of today's 'Anything on the ticker tape today?' Only the method is changed, not the basic situation. When the Roman church was a dominant temporal power, it had an unique readymade communications network throughout christendom. The British merchant venturers later became the instigators of a system of reporting back to 'head office' which provided them with swift passage of news. Exploration and colonisation led to further expansion of trade. Increased trade brought more wealth, which in turn led to the development of better banking facilities. Today, from the Bank of England to the merchant banks, all still collect and disseminate information on the economic and financial climate.

The eighteenth century saw the establishment of the Stock Exchange and all the other 'changes for the basic commodities, where the actual material or commodity was not physically present.

The role of shipping in the growth of British overseas trade was of prime importance. Hence the rise of institutions such as Lloyds of London. Insurance can only be a viable transaction when those who arrange it are in possession of as many facts as possible on the condition of the voyages. *Lloyd's list* was compiled and first issued to fulfil this need. Financial papers today have a parallel purpose. They relate the significant commercial and business events at home and abroad.

The Industrial Revolution shifted the emphasis of wealth away from the land into the cities. The main centres for rapid growth were the North West, the Midlands, Yorkshire, the North East and London. Commercial and technical information was needed in all these centres. It is significant that major libraries were set up in these areas to serve the needs of industry and commerce. The tradition of information for the business man is strong in these regions. Chambers of commerce were also founded, arising out of the need for local industry to speak with authority and unity. These too became centres for the collection and dissemination of information.

Throughout history, commercial intelligence, which includes economic, financial and social information, has been the life blood of trade and commerce. The institutions of the business world—the stock exchanges, the banks, credit worthiness agencies, insurers, company specialists—all tended to increase the need for the collection and supply of accurate, up-to-date information. Modern business and commercial information services are the latest examples of that intelligence. The methods used are the up dated version of the manuscript report now so carefully preserved as archives. Will computer programmes be as zealously collected or as reverently preserved in the twenty second century?

The present structure

The structure of commercial and business information services is not a formal one either in the UK or USA. At no point in the past has there been a conscious plan to ensure that all parts of the country will have the benefit of such services. Development has been in response to local economic need and all too often individual initiative. Provision is patchy, and many gaps remain to be filled.

National scene

The major institution of the library world in the United Kingdom is the British Library (1) (2) operating in two distinct sections. In London there are the research and reference facilities in the British Library Reference Division, the Science Reference Library, and Newspaper Library (Colindale). The lending services are provided by the British Library Lending Division at Boston Spa, Yorkshire. From the business and commercial information point of view, the British Library's copyright collection (formerly B M Library) of all books published in the UK is an authoritative and permanent source of titles.

As yet, directories, yearbooks and other commercial and business information sources are not maintained as a specific collection for the use of industry and commerce. No dissemination or enquiry service based on these books is at present envisaged as a function of the British Library. The resources of the former Patent Office Library, now renamed British Library's Science Reference Library, consist of valuable collections of scientific and technical periodicals and books which are available to the public. The library has a large staff of information workers able to help the enquirer. The Patent Office makes available their *Index to world trade marks* on 5″ × 3″ paper slips, consisting of the names which appear in the publication *Trade marks journal*. Trade catalogues are also included in the Science Reference Library's stock as part of its back up service for the patents collection. The problem of collecting trade literature has not been rationalised on a national basis. At local level too, despite specialised collections, trade literature is rarely adequately covered. This is an area where there is scope for considerable improvement.

The British Library Lending Division (3) (4) at Boston Spa is the most important loan collection of monographs and periodicals in the United Kingdom. The division brings together the resources of the former National Lending Library and the book stock and functions of the former London based National Central Library. Although originally a scientific and technically based collection, the BLLD's policy is now to cover 'all worthwhile English language books and worthwhile serials' in the fields of sociology, economics and the humanities as well as in science and technology. Loan copies of market research reports are instances of items now being made available which were formerly very difficult to obtain. Coverage of trade and commercial periodicals is also improving. The effect of the BLLD on the library scene has been dramatic.

The lack of comparable loan facilities provided at national level in the USA has restricted the growth of interlibrary lending, while the success of the British Library Lending Division in the UK has had the effect of stimulating demand for its services on a world wide basis. The publication by the Library of Congress of the *National union catalog* has been a major factor in the support of interlibrary lending in the USA.

The facilities of the Library of Congress are similar in many respects to those of the British Library Reference Division, although the American national library has had the advantage of receiving four copies of all copyright deposit titles, which it has had the right to dispose of in any way including the use for exchange purposes. Acquisition of foreign material as the result of extensive exchange arrangements has enabled the Library of Congress to achieve a rapid rate of growth with annual accessions of a quarter of a million volumes a year. Materials have been acquired from many of the overseas underdeveloped countries using currency credited from the sale of US Department of Agriculture food surpluses.

A highly important aspect of the Library of Congress services of interest to the industrial and business community is the National Referral Center for Science and Technology. Set up in 1962 it acts as a clearing house for scientific and technical enquiries, putting organisations in touch with the best service able to assist in the resolution of their problems. To facilitate this objective it undertakes a publishing programme of directories and other listings of scientific and technical information services.

Government department libraries and information services

The most extensive library information service provided by any government department for businessmen in the UK are those of the Department of Industry. (5) (6) (7) Prior to 1974 it was called Department of Trade and Industry which, in turn, was formed from an amalgamation of the Board of Trade and some parts of the earlier Ministry of Technology. The main headquarters library in Victoria Street is intended for the use of civil servants and ministers, but many of its valuable services do help other information workers to identify titles, series or references which can then be obtained from elsewhere. Each section and special agency within the Department of Industry has its own information unit. The Export Intelligence Service, with its computerised dissemination of export information, is an important example of such a unit. The Statistics and Market Intelligence Library (SMIL) in Ludgate Hill is a library with much to offer the business community. This public reference library has material on overseas markets, including large collections of economic, trade and general statistics, catalogues of foreign manufacturers, overseas development plans, and overseas trade and telephone directories. SMIL has done a remarkable job over the recent years in making export orientated information generally available. Indeed the helpfulness of its staff has made it a 'first choice' enquiry point, although some of the enquiries and requests made to SMIL could be answered from other less central information units. The businessman's lack of awareness of local commercial information sources is an unfortunate indictment of the poor 'public relations' efforts of local public libraries.

The Department of Industry has regional offices where staff are able to advise local industrialists of the range of services provided by the department. As no attempt has been made in these regional offices to establish comprehensive library services, businessmen are still well advised to deal directly with SMIL for certain of their information needs.

The local expertise and knowledge of the Department of Industry officers is a valuable asset however, and, in certain respects, regional offices can provide guidance to local sources of information of which businessmen may not always be fully aware. Providing that other libraries liaise effectively with the Department of Industry, there is no doubt that their offices can provide a useful linking role between the information services of an area. It is therefore the responsibility of individual librarians to bring their services to the notice of the Department of Industry.

The Department of Industry's regional office network is now supplemented by the Small Firm's Information Centres. Ten centres were opened in provincial cities by 1973. They are still at an experimental stage of development. They are intended to act as signposts to the correct government and other main sources of information. They are not information units as such.

The businessman will need to have dealings with many government departments other than the Department of Industry, eg, Customs and Excise, Department of Employment, etc. Each of these civil service departments has its own library and information services, but in every case, they are for the use of civil service staff and government ministers, not for the general public. There are however, certain services such as the loan service of VDI's Richtlinien from the Department of Industry, or the Technical Reports Centre's standards service from St Mary Cray, which are used directly by industry. Apart from a general willingness to be helpful whenever possible, there is no set pattern for government departments dealing with the public. There is a need for improved enquiry services in the ministries so that the public, the business and commercial enquirer, can more easily identify the relevant section of the department for his needs.

In the USA the library service of the US Department of Commerce, which had its foundations in the Department of Treasury in 1823, has built up extensive and significant historical collections during its long existence. Primarily serving the personnel of the Department of Commerce, the library does serve the general public in a very limited manner when other library sources have failed. Other literature services of special interest to the businessman are provided by the department through its Bureau of Foreign Commerce, and the US Trade Reference Room.

Local authority library services

As early as 1849 when a select committee (8) was appointed to advise on the establishment of free public libraries which culminated in the Public Libraries Act of 1850, evidence had been given suggesting the need for public commercial libraries. The Hamburg Commercial Library was cited in support of the idea of providing information services to the commercial community. Edward Edwards, later to

18

be City Librarian of Manchester, described the Hamburg library, originally established in 1835, as 'a model of what a library upon commerce ought to be'. Another witness stated that 'in the manufacturing towns of the United Kingdom, the existence of libraries connected with manufacturers in commerce would produce great advantages, not only imparting general instruction, but also in promoting the extension of the commerce and manufactures of the towns'. It was not until 1872 (9) (10) however that the first commercial library was established in the City of London. This was followed very much later by special departments created in Glasgow in 1916, Liverpool in 1917 and Manchester in 1919. These were followed by many of the other larger cities with either separate commercial libraries or, more often, with joint commercial and technical libraries, the first such library opening in Leeds in 1918. By 1924, there is evidence of the existence of no fewer than twenty four commercial collections in public libraries and seventy industrial collections (11) although many were not separately organised parts of the service. Most cities had created such services in the inter war years.

Progress over the next twenty five years was slow. Most of the larger cities and county boroughs developed good reference services and had included some form of commercial library section even if they were unable to provide a separate commercial or joint commercial and technical library. The principal restrictions which inhibited faster growth were the traditional problems of lack of financial resources, space and lack of staff. The staff aspect was further complicated by the lack of training opportunities in commercial library methods as there were few librarians with sufficient specialist skills, and no formal training courses or examinations in commercial information work were provided for in the professional syllabus.

There was considerably more expansion in the 1950's in the cities where most developments had so far occurred, and also, for the first time, in the county libraries. The first county library service was established in Lancashire in 1951, although it was almost entirely technical in character, deliberately excluding directories from its terms of reference. Other counties followed suit, but it was not until 1965 that Hertfordshire established a separate commercial section in its new branch at Stevenage which was to serve the whole county area.

During the 1950's and early 1960's (12) most public library

authorities devoted more attention to technical library services than to commercial libraries, encouraged by the boom in scientific and technical research and the national enthusiasm for nuclear and space research. These developments were matched by the existence of patent deposit collections and, later, by atomic energy deposit collections in many public libraries. This emphasis on scientific and technical literature may have been misplaced. The limited resources available to public libraries could have been used more effectively, and made a greater contribution to the economic welfare of the community, if they had concentrated on commercial library services. These, unlike scientific and technical libraries, were not provided by any other local agencies, with the exception of some chambers of commerce. This realisation may have been responsible for the improvement of public library commercial provision in the late 1960's and early 1970's which was marked, along with other developments, by the opening of a greatly expanded City Business Library at Guildhall, London (13) in 1970, Sheffield's Business Library in 1971, and Birmingham's Quick Reference Business Library in 1973. As the result of these expansions, there were considerable improvements in stock, staffing and availability of resources.

In the USA the first public commercial library was established in Newark, New Jersey by John Cotton Dana in 1904, becoming the first separate business branch only three years later. Other cities developed similar collections soon after, Minneapolis (1916), Rochester (1917), Indianapolis (1918), Detroit (1920). Cleveland, which developed such services as late as 1929, has earned a world wide reputation for its business library located in its central library as has the Kirkstein Business branch of Boston which was opened in 1930.

By 1942 at least sixty five cities with populations of over 70,000 were identified as having special library services for the business community, of which eight had separate business information departments in their central libraries, or separate business branches.

Some US public libraries have chosen to establish separate business libraries as branches in the commercial sectors of their cities. The advantages of proximity to the business users have to be offset against the problems of remoteness from the support of other central library reference facilities in related subject areas. Where the lending function in the subject area is combined with reference and information services, the former activity is often the poor relation,

20

relatively little used in comparison to that of other more centralised lending facilities. The gradual movement of business activity has caused problems as in Newark where the library, established as early as 1909 in what was then the principal business community is now at a disadvantage due to the drift of the main commercial centre away from the library. More recently, business libraries have been built in Philadelphia where the Mercantile Library shares accommodation with a busy branch library about two miles removed from the central library. Similarly in Brooklyn, where more than half of a new purpose built library in Brooklyn Heights is devoted to one of the best business reference services in the country. Despite its location in a predominantly residential district this library was the main public library business information service in New York attracting enquiries from an area much wider than the Borough of Brooklyn, until New York Public library opened the Business and Economic library of E 40th Street, adjacent to the central library, providing a much needed information service in central New York.

The present scene

From April 1974, the number of public library authorities has been reduced to 117, compared with 385 prior to local government reorganisation. This smaller number of library authorities should mean that in future, greater financial resources will lead to the availability of more specialised library materials. This, in turn, should help to improve the quality of commercial library services, together with the other specialised facilities offered by local library authorities.

The dependence of medium sized library authorities on the resources of a few major commercial reference libraries has, in effect, given regional status to some of the former county borough commercial libraries. In the past, no regional finance existed to help these major collections, although these libraries have for many years served areas much wider than the boundaries of their own local authorities. Local government reorganisation has had the effect of leaving most of these services in metropolitan districts with the result that, in many cases, the same situation exists as before reorganisation. A few metropolitan districts are supplying the reference and information services and providing an in depth supporting role to the surrounding conurbations, without any compensating financial arrangements. There is no doubt that consideration will have to be given to this problem, which might be overcome by finance from central government funds or by agency payments from county councils responsible for the first tier services in the areas concerned.

Of the local authorities in the London region, the outstanding commercial reference service is that of the City Business Library. The City Business Library grew out of the Commercial Reference Room of the Guildhall Library of the City of London. In its fine new building, it provides a good all round service with a first class collection of material for the businessman. Westminster City Library's Central Reference Library, Camden Public Library's St Pancras and Holborn Commercial Reference Libraries, Lambeth Public Library are major commercial collections. Many other London borough libraries provide smaller commercial information services. In the main, however, the business and commercial information needs of London and the South East still depend on the City Business Library, the Statistics and Market Intelligence Library, and on some of the services available on a commercial basis which are mentioned below.

Outside London, commercial reference libraries are inevitably concentrated in the main industrial and commercial centres. Manchester Commercial Library (14) (15) is acknowledged to be the model of a well run and long established information unit to serve industry and the businessman. Its internationally high reputation is based on a well trained staff plus a very comprehensive collection concentrated on quick reference materials, including statistics, directories, periodicals and indexes. A notable part of its service is the selection of international financial and trade newspapers. Birmingham's new central library contains a special Quick Reference Business Library, sited near the main entrance to encourage ease of access for the local business community. Here too, the provision of commercial material is good, and the staff ratio sufficient to ensure an in depth service. Other public libraries with separate business and commercial libraries include Sheffield, Glasgow, and Liverpool. Combined commercial and technical reference departments in local authority libraries are long standing features of Nottingham, Bristol, Leeds, Newcastle, Hull and Coventry. One of the strengths of these public library services to commerce and industry is their local knowledge and their local expertise. Each provides a general service to the business community, plus that extra concern for the special needs of the region. Many of these libraries have become nationally known for a particular service or subject, such as Leeds, with its well organised international patents collection, Sheffield and its *World metal index*, Birmingham and its company information indexes and Manchester with its indexes of statistical sources. Special information services such as these deserve wider support and recognition, both to maintain and encourage their existence, and also to prevent the needless duplication of effort by other libraries in other regions.

The contrast between the size of public library authorities is even greater in the USA than it was in the UK before reorganisation. Over 7,000 public library authorities exist, of which only the largest are able to sustain fully comprehensive business information services. Nonetheless, it has been suggested that even the smaller library authorities should become an integral part of a business firm's information support system. Meyer and Rostvold (23) recommended that 'a public library should take on the role of being the first point of contact for the businessman who does not have his own company library but who needs some information.' The report based on two small Californian towns, stresses the contribution which can be made by the small authority in this respect.

Significant differences exist in the types of material provided by American and British business libraries. The former are strong on the provision of financial information services, corporation report files, bibliographical tools in economics and commerce and cutting files. In the UK, much greater stress is laid on the provision of up-to-date and comprehensive directory collections both national and foreign, particularly where overseas markets are concerned.

Additional facilities available in many American libraries include coin operated typewriters and a much wider provision of coin operated photocopying machines.

Academic library services
The creation of information services within university libraries is a comparatively recent development. University libraries have unrivalled book and periodical collections but their use by the businessman or industrialist is only now beginning to be possible. Warwick University has led the way with its statistical collection based on the back files of the Statistics and Market Intelligence Library's extensive range of titles. It can be used, on a subscription basis, by outside organisations. The establishment of two major business schools—in London and Manchester—has also made definitive collections of management books, periodicals and related materials available in those cities. Both business schools

have excellent libraries which include items such as company reports and company share card services. The library and information service is an integral part of the London Business School's courses. It encourages, as a matter of policy, the use of the library as an information source by its old students. In its publications, the information needs of the student and research worker are constantly stressed. Bradford University has a business and management studies department and another major collection in this field is maintained at the Cranfield Polytechnic.

From 1973, the remaining industrial liaison officers are now based on the polytechnics as members of departments directly concerned with industry. They do not aim to provide an information service but rather a practical problem solving service using the skills and knowledge available within the polytechnics. They have established wide ranging contacts with all sections of local business and trade, together with a knowledge of information and advisory services in government departments, research associations and nationalised industries. As an initial point of enquiry for the firm requiring advice on production or technological problems, the industrial liaison officer offers a different kind of service from other information agencies.

The recent development of the British graduate business schools reflected the success of the older established American business schools. Harvard Graduate School of Business Administration (founded in 1926) is the largest school of its kind in the USA. It's size is reflected by the Baker library divided into five divisions, with a stock of half a million volumes. In addition to a main reference department, there are divisions devoted to corporation records, an important library of early books on business and economics published before 1630 in the Kress library, a manuscript and archives division and a reading room of recreational material for business school students.

The Massachusetts Institute of Technology Library (MIT) library also contains an important Management and Social Sciences Library with 250,000 volumes covering economics, management, marketing, finance, banking, sociology, and industrial relations, the latter an important special collection in its own right.

Interlibrary cooperation
The recognition that no library 'is an island' has resulted in the de-

velopment, within the spheres of industry and commerce, of very active cooperation between all types of library and information units on a regional basis. Commercial information sections of the larger library services are partners in these cooperatives. The growth of the cooperative schemes has been well documented. (16)-(20)

SINTO (Sheffield Interchange Organisation) was the first cooperative scheme to be established in 1932. (16) By the end of the 1960's many other similar schemes had come into being, including HULTIS (Hull), LADSIRLAC (Liverpool), CICRIS (Acton), SASLIC (Surrey and Sussex), CADIG (Coventry), HERTIS (Hertfordshire), HATRICS (Southampton), NANTIS (Nottingham), BRASTACS (Bradford). There are now about 24 schemes in active existence, each unique in its structure and organisation, with the major differences being in their methods of finance. Originally many of the schemes concentrated on the problems of local provision of periodicals, hence the large number of union lists of periodicals which were issued. With the advent of the National Lending Library, now the British Library Lending Division, this need becomes less pressing. The cooperative schemes are now generally more concerned with the information needs of their areas. They fulfil a training function through seminars and courses, act as coordinating networks for special librarians and information officers, and provide a professional backup service for information units of all sizes. Library cooperative schemes are important in the structure of business and commercial information services because they make it possible to focus the attention of all types of library within the area on the resources of others, and help to make those resources more widely available. All this is achieved in a voluntary and friendly manner. Although a large number of libraries in the United Kingdom are supported by public funds (local authorities, universities, polytechnics, government departments), it is only at the level of cooperative schemes that an overall look can be taken of the information needs of each local community.

The Standing Conference of Cooperative Library Information Services (SCOCLIS) was founded in 1964, but it has never achieved the role as coordinator of library cooperative services which was envisaged by its founders. The joint indexing of *Jordans daily list of new companies* from 1965 to 1973 has been one of its few significant projects. A dozen major reference libraries combined to produce this index which was quarterly with annual cumulations. The *Daily list* ceased publication in its original form in 1973. The index was a truly cooperative venture, indicative of the potential scope for practical interlibrary cooperation. Since this date access to currently registered details of private companies are no longer available from any library in the United Kingdom. Data on new company registrations is available to personal applicants to Companies House, or to subscribers to the Manuscript Transcription Service, organised by Jordan's. Birmingham's Quick Reference Business Library is still endeavouring to maintain its long-standing files of company information.

In 1972, the formation of the Library Association Reference, Special and Information Section Working Party on Business Information, made it possible for librarians from every type of library involved in commercial information work to consider business information provision and problems. One of its first tasks was to investigate how comprehensively European company information was covered by the major business reference libraries. Its preliminary survey showed that although many libraries had most of the major publications, there was still a significant number of important foreign sources of information which were not available anywhere in the United Kingdom. Very little is known of the exact nature of the commercial information resources available either in London or the regional business libraries.

Chambers of commerce
The information and library services of the British chambers of commerce are usually restricted to members only. Across the country, the standard of services varies considerably in respect to the quality of their information services. The London Chamber of Commerce library is outstandingly good and its information service is widely acclaimed as an important source of aid for business and commerce. Other notable chambers of commerce with library services are Birmingham, Leicester and Liverpool. There is room for improved cooperation between the chambers of commerce and the other information giving organisations within each area. Where chambers take part in local cooperative schemes their membership can make a significant contribution to local library cooperation. It is here that such schemes are important with their across-the-board sphere of influence. Because of the uncoordinated nature of business information services, there is occasionally almost conflict (at least there is

rivalry) between the different agencies providing the services. Some general enquiries made by out of town readers not familiar with the appropriate information agency are often addressed to 'Information. Blanktown'. The address to which such an enquiry is delivered by the post office can often reveal the relative public consciousness of the services provided by the public library, the chamber of commerce or the municipal information service.

The chamber of commerce movement has spread all over the world. In the United Kingdom, apart from the British chambers, there are the two-nation chambers of commerce, such as the Netherlands British Chamber of Commerce, the Swedish Chamber of Commerce for the UK or the American Chamber of Commerce in the UK. These are ancillary sources of information on export markets, and economic conditions in foreign countries. Many of these two-nation chambers issue yearbooks or directories. Each one differs from the others in the form of its information service. Many of these chambers of commerce have strong links with the commercial departments of their respective embassies and also with the industries of their home countries.

Banks

In the course of their day to day activities, banks amass a considerable amount of economic, financial and political intelligence. Although all major banks have fully organised information sections for their own internal use, their importance to the flow of business information in the wider sense is through their numerous and well researched special publications. Public commercial libraries and the business information coverage in special libraries are well served by the various economic reports such as *Barclays review*, or Lloyds Bank, *Economic reports* on individual countries.

In the USA the World Bank in Washington houses the joint library of the International Monetary Fund at the International Bank for Reconstruction and Development founded when the World Bank was created in 1946. The library contains over 100,000 volumes concentrating on government publications, foreign trade and statistics from all countries.

World trade centre

A recent development on the international business scene is the plan to set up World Trade Centres, in which there are facilities for business activity, and, incidentally, for recreation. A World Trade Centre's main function is the provision of services, generally under the same roof. The facilities include general forms of assistance (secretarial, translating, telex,) and more specialised functions (commercial intelligence, communications media). Computer facilities in the various World Trade Centres are compatible in terms of systems and hardware. Facsimile transmission equipment will be incorporated into the communications package available.

The object of the World Trade Centres is to speed up the provision of commercial information, using a computer information bank named *Interfile*. *Interfile* seeks to provide a data bank collection, having access to a wide range of trade information extracted from government publications, periodicals, books, etc to which is added local information from the growing number of World Trade Centres. The *Interfile* service is most highly developed in the United States of America, where it operates as an on line shared computer retrieval bank from a central data bank in Cleveland. The London version of *Interfile* is still at the planning stage.

The Institute of Export has transferred its library services to the London World Trade Centre to form the nucleus of the WTC's comprehensive reference library. The classification scheme to be used will be the same as that used for *Interfile*. It is claimed that there will be no unnecessary duplication of services by the London WTC and the existing information services, such as the Statistics and Market Intelligence Library, the Export Intelligence Service of the Department of Industry, or the chambers of commerce.

Embassies
The library and information services of foreign embassies in the United Kingdom provide varying levels of service. Some of the embassies have extensive facilities, although they are not always willing to make their services available to the general enquirer.

Many of the general requests received by such libraries are often capable of being dealt with by other information agencies, and this may account for the attitude of some of the embassies to these enquiries and their unwillingness to handle them. But embassy libraries, together with the resources of their commercial attaches, have access to extensive commercial information sources. If approached tactfully in relevant cases, embassies are potentially important sources of information.

The German and Japanese embassies fully realise the importance of providing information, and the French Embassy is very active. Some of the smaller nations have not yet appreciated that their embassies have an important role to play in giving information to British industry. The United States Information Services have been much reduced in recent years, with the unfortunate result that American information is more difficult to trace.

Research and trade associations

The research associations, with their responsibilities confined to individual subject areas, now number approximately forty. In the past, activities have largely been limited to carrying out pure and applied research in the furtherance of industrial development. But there are significant changes of direction now in progress. Their libraries have also changed to reflect the new pattern. Some have expanded their activities in recent years to embrace commercial information activities. The Rubber and Plastics Research Association for example, has for many years published a number of guides to commercial information sources, including the annual *New trade names in the rubber and plastics industries* which has become an important reference source. RAPRA's Economics Information Unit has also developed a wide range of commercial services and supplementary publications and they have plans to expand this side of their activity more in the future. (21) Unlike public service or government libraries, the first responsibility of research and trade associations has to be to their members, and, understandably, many are wary of making their knowledge available to non-members. They are still a highly important part of the business and commercial information services of the United Kingdom. Their involvment with economic and business information is bound to increase in the next decade.

Another useful institutional library is that of the Institute of Marketing which has an Information Services Department. This provides practical advice on every aspect of marketing, and it is able to draw on all the resources of the institute's library. Their stock is classified by the London Business School Classification scheme and includes United Kingdom consumer market surveys and American marketing practice reports.

Newspaper libraries

The *Financial times* SVP Business Information Service is a commercially based information service offering access to the business information resources of the extensive *Financial times* newspaper library. It is linked to the long established French SVP (S'il vous plait) service. Subscriptions range from £10 per month. The basic data for this service is all the information contained in the *Financial times*, or compiled from reports prepared for the *Financial times* which is reprocessed and repackaged to make it suitable for dissemination to subscribers to the service. The service has been successful, and up to a point, its expertise is in its method of selling its service, rather than in the nature of the information sold. It is an example of the intensive exploitation of an existing body of information.

Other newspaper libraries offer more general information support, although not as relevant to the interests of businessmen as the *Financial times*. They are, nonetheless, important sources of information particularly for topics of current interest and, obviously, for guidance to the content of their own newspapers. Amongst these, the *Daily telegraph* has built up a reputation for information provision and has sought to encourage the general public, and the businessman's secretary, to use their quick reference information service.

Technical help to exporters
Despite its name, this British Standards Institution's offshoot at Hemel Hempstead, (22) is steadily building up a commercial information service for the exporter based on information to be found in standards, regulations and codes of foreign standards organisations and on the detailed knowledge of commercial requirements collected by THE's information engineers. As such, it complements the facilities existing in the Department of Industry libraries and other published data based library collections. Although much of the information is outside the scope of this account, the understanding of regulations and commercial conditions of contracts is important to any commercial undertaking. THE is a subscription service. Its information is disseminated through its *THE technical digests, THE information sheets*, translations, and there is a telephone enquiry service. Increasingly as Technical Help to Exporters develops world wide contacts, it will become a major part of the information for the businessman.

Chapter 2

Organisation and administration: objectives planning and staffing

A Leslie Smyth

The objectives of a business library have probably never been more lucidly propounded than by Stanley Jast in 1919. 'The aim of this library may be concisely stated as the provision of any and every kind of commercial information which may be obtained from printed matter, and such additional information as it may be possible to procure from public or private sources; the collection, arrangement and cataloguing of such printed matter so as to render it quickly and conveniently available for enquirers and readers'.(1)

A parallel interpretation of function was made by Lord Parmoor at the opening of the Liverpool Commercial Library, in 1917. 'I look upon this library as doing the liaison work between research on the one side and practical business on the other . . . This library is not a school of commerce; it is not a place for you to learn commerce, but it is a place where people who are skilled in commerce may go to obtain information of a wide kind which they may want in connection with their business.' (2)

Jast's perceptive views contrast with the rigid theories held by Lamb (3) writing over thirty years later, in which a business library is regarded basically as an allocation of classification numbers in the apportionment of a complete classification system between subject departments. (Thus Lamb considers certain Dewey numbers appropriate to a business library eg 333.6 but not 333.7, 334.2 but not 334.8, 338.5 but not 338.6). From an administrative point of view, this gives no untidy subject overlap between departments but it is stultifying for the development of an active business library.

There are four important elements in Jast's concept which are crucial to the running of a well organised business library.

1 The wide range of printed sources of information, both in subject coverage and physical form.

2 The procurement of non-printed information which could include anything from a press hand-out to information received orally.

3 A quick and convenient service made possible by the arrangement of material in ways perhaps not acceptable to the more conventionally organised library.

4 The emphasis on 'enquirers' as well as 'readers' with the implication that the staff are to provide answers direct to readers without necessarily the interposition of the written word.

To these should be added two further essentials neatly expressed by Rose Vainstein.(4)

5 Publicity should be continuous and specific and advantage should be taken of all media of communication.

6 Business trends and interests should be anticipated and community contacts should be close and diverse.

In practice, a business library operates on two levels of service. Firstly, providing a quick reference service on commercial as well as general topics. Secondly, a more specialised service covering company information, marketing, insurance, investment, exporting, advertising, management and similar subjects of particular interest to business. The whole emphasis is on contemporary conditions, with retrospective information usually left to other library departments to provide.

Use

There have been few objective studies of the use and users of business libraries. The two most notable are Meyer and Rostvold's market analysis of information needs of business and industry in two medium sized communities in California (5) and the Aslib research department's pilot study of use and users of the Manchester Commercial Library (6). Some of the findings of the latter have application to business libraries generally and include:

1 A large proportion of a business library's clientele came from a much wider area than that of the authority financing the service. The Aslib study found that the workplaces of 33% of personal visitors and 59% of telephone callers were outside the authority boundaries.

from public pressures can also become a problem area.

There are obviously many potential points of friction in dealing with support departments and the business librarian is unwise to delegate too much in these contacts. For example, pressure must be exerted on the book ordering department to obtain material quickly, maintain standing orders efficiently, chase up outstanding orders regularly and give a certain priority in processing. Obviously, this requires continual personal involvement and a large measure of diplomacy. It is advantageous to get staff in support departments to take a personal interest in the business library and make them aware of the importance of their particular job to the service provided.

Planning

The usual location of a business library is at the centre of a large conurbation although, with new urban transport conditions and developments in telecommunications, this may not be so in the future. At present, a central situation in the business area of a large city adjacent to transport and parking facilities is the ideal.

Some libraries such as Birmingham, Liverpool and Manchester have had experience of premises separate from their central libraries whilst the cities of London, Glasgow and Dublin still operate in this way. There is an obvious conflict between the advantages of a good business site and the opportunities afforded by what has been called the hinterland of information provided by other departments in the same building. (7) Whether on its own or not, the business library should be clearly identifiable; illuminated signs and display windows are an obvious advantage. It should be on the ground floor with easy access from the street.

In considering the lay-out of the floor area of the library itself, a major factor must be the maintenance of a rapid information service both to the personal caller and the telephone inquirer. If stock is too dispersed, then the time taken by staff to walk to source material becomes an unacceptably large component in the time needed to provide an answer. There is obviously a critical size for the floor area occupied by this material which should be as near to the inquiry counter as possible and not interspersed by reading tables. Short stay consultation does not usually require seating accommodation and provision should be made accordingly. The user engaged in more lengthy and concentrated study should be separated from the inevitable bustle and noise around the inquiry area and facilities for the public to use telephones, tape-recorders, adding machines and type-writers must be taken into account in the acoustical planning of the department. Flexibility is the key-note in the lay-out, with inspiration from the retail store rather than the reference library. Access to material should be made as quick and simple as possible by generous provision of signing and guiding.

The inquiry counter

In an information department, the inquiry counter is the pivot of the whole organisation. It must be situated close to the entrance, uncluttered, well illuminated and designed as an obvious focal point. A horse-shoe shape, with the open end backing on to the stack, work room, telephone and telex areas, is very suitable. There must be ample accommodation for card indexes and books frequently required to answer inquiries (there will be duplicate copies of these on the public shelves). Photocopying equipment is best located at the further side of the counter from the entrance so that people requiring this service are separated from those wanting information. The non-public stacks house unbound newspaper and periodical files, older and superseded stock and items at risk on the public shelves.

Few libraries have made anything but casual provision for an efficient telephone information service. Users in person and telephone inquiries are normally dealt with at the same counter, with the unsatisfactory result that simultaneous demands either leave the telephones unanswered or the person waiting at the counter feeling he is being ignored. In both the DTI Statistics and Market Intelligence Library and the Birmingham Quick Reference and Commercial Library staff answering telephone inquiries are seated at desks away from the public resulting in a more relaxed atmosphere in which to concentrate on the inquiry and adequate desk space for the consultation of material. Birmingham also has the central switchboard for inquiries to all departments in this area, with the advantage that the operator is able to consult the professional staff when deciding where to route an inquiry. When telephones are attended to by counter staff, coloured light rather than bell signals should be installed and the telephones themselves housed on a ledge separate from the surface where material is consulted.

The Cleveland Business Information Department* provides a

* The information on Cleveland Business Information Department has been kindly communicated by Miss Agnes Hanson to whom the author is indebted.

separate telephone desk pragmatically designed to meet the requirements of a busy inquiry service. It is situated a few feet away from the main reference inquiry counter and seats a couple of not too portly librarians side by side. At the front is a grilled locked case topped by a ledge deep enough for materials to be examined on it. Above is a glass noise screen encircling the telephone desk on three sides. Behind are two broad sections of shelving in the wall space, the exact length of the telephone desk, so that the staff have just to reach back for the most used volumes shelved there. On the lower shelf is a phalanx of high use city 'phone books which in Cleveland's case includes Montreal, Toronto and the London commercial. At the staff's fingertips on top of the desk, there are duplicate copies of *Moody's industrials, Thomas' register, MacRae's blue book, Poor's register,* Dun and Bradstreet's directories and *Standard directory of advertisers* whilst on the shelf below are local directories such as *Cleveland buyers' guide* and *Ohio directory of manufacturers.*

The telephone desk is flanked at both ends by back-to-back catalogue stands containing domestic card indexes eg, order files, reference aid files, consumer index, author index to subject file pamphlets and trade catalogue index. The main reference desk, which also has a telephone, borrows from the telephone desk when needed and both desks are planned so that they can be run by reduced staff in the evening slack periods.

Furniture and fittings
The nature of the stock of a business library and the arrangements for providing a rapid information service mean that special consideration must be given to furniture and fittings. (8) The requirements of particular kinds of stock are as follows:

Directories Bearing in mind that much of the use of directories is for brief references to often heavy volumes, directory stands should have ledges for consultation at least 35 cms wide and about 90 cms from the floor. There will be five shelves to each stand at least 35 cms apart with the two lower shelves built out to project the same distance as the ledge. Stands of this kind do not appear to be available from the usual library furniture suppliers but, if space is not limited, then three book shelves and a reference shelf can be substituted. One of the advantages of this arrangement is that, as well as economising in seating accommodation, directories are usually replaced after use and not dispersed over various tables, an important factor in maintaining an information service in a busy library.

Company card services Publishers of company card services can supply the necessary filing cabinets with the requisite number of drawers. Moodies British Company Service fits into a 100 × 60 cms freestanding three drawer cabinet with each drawer sub-divided to accommodate the 22 × 18 cms annual cards and the 17 × 11 cms news cards. Alternatively, the cards can be filed in 22 × 18 cms sheaf folders (as in the City Business Library) which have all the advantages of book form. Extel provide lateral cabinets containing various numbers of 20 × 12 cms drawers depending on the range of services taken. McCarthy's cards are similar in size and can be housed in the same way. Cabinets may be placed on an ordinary reading table which allows a space for consultation or else accommodated in a specially made rack. Annual reports of companies are best kept in cardboard filing boxes on ordinary folio shelving, although rotary filing equipment is also used.

Vertical file When the public have direct access, a suspended filing system in metal cabinets is preferable to lateral filing. The individual files should have the contents heading extending across the whole width of the file when an alphabetico-classed arrangement is used. The contents of each drawer should be detailed on two 25 × 10 cms panels on the front of the drawer, as the normal contents card is not large enough for public display; most manufacturers will add the necessary slots at a small extra cost. The cabinets can be usefully placed on a raked dais, about 15 cms high, to improve ease of consultation.

Maps Maps have been appropriately described as 'librarians' problem children' and the accepted difficulties of storage, preservation and retrieval are heightened by concentrated use and the necessity for speedy availability. (9) These issues are further compounded when the public have direct access and a single map browser can leave a long trail of misplaced and untidily filed sheets. In spite of the security risk, folded maps are to be preferred and the OS 1:50,000 sheets can be accommodated in this form on ordinary shelving whilst folded town plans can be housed in filing boxes or cabinets. The City Business Library has a display of maps on hinged metal frames. (10) Although vertical filing of map sheets has some advantages, on balance horizontal filing in flat drawer metal plan files is to be preferred. Heavily used series, such as the local 1:1,250 plans, can be bought guarded on the western edge of each sheet and kept in loose-leaf screw binders. A special map table is essential when there is extensive use of maps; this table can also incorporate storage for the larger atlases.

Periodicals Periodical racks should be chosen to give the maximum display possible. The typical business user browses through a greater number of periodicals and over a wider range of subjects than his technical or scientific colleague who is often primarily concerned with individual titles. For this reason, periodicals are better arranged by subject groups than alphabetically by title. Newspapers present particular problems of space and display; the modern newspaper wall-racks, although not a complete answer, seem to present the best solution.

Pamphlets A large proportion of business stock is in pamphlet form which when normally housed, has poor display potential. Peg board screens can be used with great advantage to display new material.

Staff
An information service stands or falls according to the quality of its staff and, because of a number of factors, the calibre of staff of a business service is even more crucial than in ordinary reference work. As a result of the instability of business information, there are problems in handling—published sources are continually changing; the data available is often 'uncooked'; there is a lack of an adequate bibliographical framework with the usual guides, bibliographies and indexes; the physical form of material is diverse. Equally challenging is the need to work under pressure without the time to make a thorough literature search and yet with the knowledge that the facts required are often of great importance to the enquirer. It calls for a flair for the unusual approach together with a flexibility of mind in solving inquiries. It requires a knowledge of business events (obtained from a daily reading of the *Financial times*) which enables staff to anticipate enquiries and, equally important, to be on the same wave length as users. Effective oral communication is a prime necessity and, whilst many inquirers are unable to express themselves adequately, equally many inexperienced staff are unable to listen and formulate clearly what is required.

Ideally, staff should have a general reference background with an intimate and extensive acquaintance with business library material.

They must know of outside sources, particularly those in the immediate locality. It is often overlooked that this data is built up by the teamwork of an enthusiastic staff and that many inquiries are answered, without recourse to printed matter, from the card information file or from the personal knowledge of the individual member of staff.

All this demands from staff a high degree of commitment and, in return, they should be given considerable freedom and trust. Paradoxically, in this situation, it is more important than ever that each person's responsibilities in the running of the library should be clearly defined. Although supervision must be discreet and unobtrusive, it must nevertheless be there particularly when certain staff do not meet the high standards required.

The smooth running of any library is dependent on efficient routine carried out with precision. This becomes of supreme importance where there is a rapid turnround of stock and that stock includes tens of thousands of clippings, index cards, company service cards, sheet maps and plans, cyclostyled sheets, yearbooks, reports, pamphlets and amendment pages. Not only is this true in the daily filing of new items which forms a large part of the routine of any business library but also in the replacement of material after use. It is much easier to re-file a company card or map sheet out of place than a bound volume. Some libraries use a full-time filing clerk for all new filing whilst others divide the filing between junior members of staff. Each is given a filing day, say once a week, with the responsibility of filing all material arriving on that day. Although not popular with staff, filing is a recuperative job after the pressures of the information desk.

Deployment of staff at any given time between information work, routine and training is dependent on the weight of use. Ideally, the person in charge of the information desk should be able to augment the initial allocation of staff by calling on the help of other members to prevent queues or delays in answering telephones.

Because of so many local variables, it is extremely difficult to suggest a staff establishment for a business library. With opening hours numbering 60–70/week, personal users 200,000–250,000/year and telephone inquiries 25,000–30,000/year, a staff of twelve would probably be needed. Of these, a minimum of a half should be qualified professionally. Any increase in the telephone inquiry service, which is highly labour intensive, would obviously require more staff. Another factor to be considered is the rate of staff turnover, often high in an urban commercial centre, and this has to be set against a background of rigid salary structure common to many local authorities.

Allocation of duties

The following is an example of the allocation of duties. All staff deal with inquiries.

Librarian: General administration of staff and bookstock, as well as relations with users. Maintenance of professional expertise and business knowledge. This is gained by constant surveillance of the financial press, knowledge of new contributions to the literature and conversations with informed users of the library.

Selection and appraisal of stock.

Organisation and management of stock; its processing, binding maintenance, display, utilisation, security and discarding.

The collection of data and its organisation, development and retrieval as information; the balance and weighting of various subjects.

The provision of a service of factual information; dealing with the more difficult inquiries referred by other members of staff.

The promotion of the library by personal contact with commercial, governmental and other organisations, speaking at meetings, arranging courses, compilation and distribution of guides, booklists and bibliographies.

Staff training and education.

Liaison with other departments of the system.

Sub-Librarian: Day-to-day staff matters.

Staff deployment.

Stock maintenance.

Map collection.

Clippings selection—*Financial times* and *Trade and industry*.

Electoral registers indexing (supervision)

Displays (supervision)

Periodicals (supervision)

Assistant librarian 1

Vertical file maintenance.

Pamphlets-indexing and classification.

Clippings selection—*Times* and *Economist*.

Supervision of company services, trade mark indexes, photocopying and special loans.

Stationery requisitioning.

Assistant librarian 2

Statistics collection-indexing and shelf-listing.

Maintenance of information file.

Clippings selection—*Guardian* and local papers.

Assistant librarian 3

Directories—indexing and shelf-listing.

Bookstock—processing and indexing.

Checking bibliographies.

Missing stock and stock-taking.

Assistant 1

Newspaper clippings—cutting, mounting and filing.

Newspaper files.

Filing correspondence.

Lost property.

Assistant 2

Company reports—checking and maintenance.

Maps—filing and maintenance.

Town plans—processing, indexing, filing and maintenance.

Assistant 3

Binding of non-periodical material

Transfers and discards.

Stack directory sequences.

Assistant 4

Information file.

Official and holiday guides—maintenance and indexing.

Timetables.

Assistant 5

Periodicals—binding, indexing, processing new titles, overdue periodicals, display.

Assistant 6

Pamphlet filing.

Photocopying.

All assistants share responsibility for filing, maintaining periodical files and straightening.

Procedure instructions

It is important that procedures should be clearly laid down for all routine jobs particularly when there is a large turnover of staff. This is achieved by having explicit procedure instructions, one for each routine, which are regularly revised. A master file is available for any member of staff to consult and personal copies of the appropriate instructions are given to those concerned with a particular routine. Examples of procedure instructions:

Extel Company Services filing (4 pages); Allocation of duties (as above) (1 page); Straightening and clearing (2 pages) Official guides (2 pages); Special loans (1 page); Responsibilities of counter senior (1 page); Registers of electors (3 pages); Photocopying (1 page); Pamphlets (2 pages); Counter routine (including telephone and telex inquiry routine) (2 pages); Cash (2 pages); Statistics collection (11 pages); Company reports (2 pages).

As an example, the main headings in the Extel Company Services filing procedure instruction are: 1 Sequences of cards; 2 Arrangement within each sequence; 3 Stamping; 4 Filing; 5 New users and placings; 6 Order of cards; 7 Maintenance of index of companies; 8 Deletions; 9 Changes of name; 10 Superseded cards.

Staff training

As in military operations, the greater the pressure under which a unit is likely to operate, the more important does adequate training become. Training falls into two distinct areas. The first covers domestic matters and routines whilst the second relates to background information and education. Examples of subjects covered are:

Domestic

1 Filing, including company card services; 2 Counter routine; 3 Telephone and telex routines; 4 Photocopying; 5 Locations of material; 6 Sessions with individual members of staff who describe their jobs and, in this way, cover the various kinds of bibliographical material; 7 Complaints and suggestions; 8 Other library departments.

Background

1 Companies; 2 Trade names; 3 Directories; 4 Maps; 5 Investment; 6 Indexes and Abstracts; 7 Official publications; 8 EC legislation; 9 Book selection.

It will be noticed that most subjects in domestic training have a corresponding procedure instruction and these are communicated in as easily digestible a form as possible, with personal interpretation and examples. Practical demonstration is preferable to verbal description and, although the way in which periodicals are prepared for binding may be carefully detailed in an instruction, the method of training would in fact consist of a demonstration of the actual work involved. The written instruction is then much easier understood and can be used for future reference.

Background training is equally important because it is not possible to answer questions competently in many business subjects without knowing something about those subjects. For example, company information abounds in pitfalls for someone who knows nothing about company registration, the statutory provision of company information or the various kinds of companies which exist. Because of the present inadequacy of business education in library schools, this kind of training is just as necessary for professionally qualified staff joining a business library as for others.

Both types of training are applicable to the same topic. Domestic consideration of directories includes shelf arrangement, local indexes, counter and stack sequences, shelf listing, classification and degree of use, whilst background training includes method of compilation, classification of products, internal indexing, national peculiarities such as alphabetisation, and standards for comparison.

Cleveland BID lays stress on orientation reference exercises in which the trainee, whether professional or pre-professional, has to answer given questions from the more used business information sources. A half day, sandwiched between desk assignments and routine duties, is usually given to answer each paper. The progression of sources is as follows:

1 *Thomas' register* and *MacRae's blue book*.

2 Dun and Bradstreet *Middle market, Million dollar* directories, *Encyclopedia of associations, Poor's register of directors and executives, Standard directory of advertisers, National trade and professional associations*.

3 Directories in special fields and foreign directories.

4 Moody's *Manuals*, Standard and Poor's *Corporation records, Financial post* manuals.

5 Introduction to statistics—*Statistical abstract, Historical statistics, Business statistics, Survey of current business*.

Examples of questions: Where are the factories of the General Signal Corp located? Find a ten-year stock price range for Lane Bryant Inc. When was the Blue Ridge Real Estate Co incorporated? Find an account of the Ohio Turnpike Commission. What dividends were paid last year by Abbott Laboratories?

In finding the answers to questions the trainee is entirely on his own but, after each set, his supervisor goes over them, helping out with any problems and showing some of the more specialised, comprehensive or alternative sources not specified in the exercise.

Whilst it is possible to give some training in elementary enquiry techniques and it is necessary to know the correct practice before taking short cuts, the actual skills of business information work can only be learnt on the job itself. Experience in dealing with inquirers, understanding people, ability to communicate, intimate knowledge of resources, power to recall information quickly, flexibility of mind, intelligent anticipation, ability to select and use material at speed, and a background awareness of events, all combined with a flair to produce the right answer rapidly and with assurance—these are the qualities of the ideal business library staff.

Bespoke service

Business information is a highly marketable commodity and it is doubtful if the public library, conditioned by lending library counter thinking, is always tuned in to the real requirements of the business community. The very surroundings where consultations are made lack the comfort and privacy to which the businessman is accustomed when he asks for information from an accountant, lawyer or government official. (In this respect, the Small Firms Information Centres provide a good example of what is required). There are many extra facilities for which business inquirers would no doubt be prepared to pay—particularly if the library service was tailored to their individual needs.

Probably the most advanced custom-designed public library research service aimed at the business community is INFORMA (Information for Minnesota). (11) This is a cooperative library endeavour begun in 1972 with four participating libraries—Minneapolis Public Library, St Paul Public Library, the James J Hill Reference Library (St Paul) and the University of Minnesota Library. A uniform search fee of $18 an hour is charged by each library and resources are made available to the subscriber beyond the traditional terms of public library service. 'Primarily the difference is that the information sought demands more exhaustive, diligent and protracted investigation requiring the examination, evaluation and summation of information obtained not only from written sources but also from nonprint media, individuals and organizations.'

Special emphasis is placed on the convenience, confidentiality and

45

flexibility of the service. Visits are made and material delivered to the customer's office and extra-mural searches are made in other libraries and government offices. When the customer visits the library, a special study carrel is available where books and periodicals are set aside, flagged with relevant references. If necessary, bibliographies can be prepared and formal reports made. The librarian assigned to this service becomes, in some ways, the temporary employee of the company. He has additional commitment because of closer knowledge of the background of an inquiry and can concentrate on a thorough and complete search to attain a satisfactory answer. Whilst it was originally envisaged that the use of the service would be limited to small firms, the majority of demand has turned out to come from large corporations, some with well developed libraries of their own.

The present growth of commercial services offering business information on demand, such as FIND, SVP, Packaged Facts and the *Financial times* information service, indicates that there is considerable scope for the public library and that John Cotton Dana's original ideas of serving the business community are capable of immense expansion.

Chapter 3

Organisation and administration: classification, cataloguing and arrangement

A Leslie Smyth

The following considerations apply in the arrangement of business material

1 Book classification schemes are unsatisfactory and inappropriate for the majority of items.

2 Stock is usually separated by physical form—directories, statistics, company services, company reports, clippings, timetables, official guides, plans, gazetteers. For speedy retrieval, a suitable scheme of arrangement is used for each form.

3 Much material is ephemeral and full cataloguing treatment is uneconomic.

4 The mechanics of using a catalogue (particularly a classed card catalogue) is too cumbersome for quick reference. A strip index is far more efficient as well as being more familiar to business users.

5 For those items which are to be permanently preserved, full classification and cataloguing with entries in the central reference catalogue is necessary. After this material ceases to have business interest, its ultimate destination will be another department of the library and a unique call number is required from the outset. Central catalogue entries also ensure that marginal interests of other departments are covered.

6 When new material is needed quickly then the fewer processes it goes through, the better. Similarly, on discarding, the tighter the bibliographical control, the more expensive the process.

7 Certain bibliographies specially compiled for business use are

more efficient than ordinary catalogues for exploiting the stock because of features such as analytical indexes. A good example is *Current British directories*; many libraries prominently display copies of this work which have been annotated with directory stand numbers and interleaved so that additions and amendments can be made.

8 Emphasis of use is on items of information rather than books. Much material containing business information has no title-page or author and lacks conventional bibliographical form. In these circumstances, staff information indexes are more appropriate than catalogues.

9 Public use of staff is proportionately greater than in other departments.

It is interesting to compare and contrast the ways in which two business libraries, the City Business Library (CBL) and Manchester Commercial Library (MCL), have solved the problems of arrangement. In some cases, the two have come to similar solutions quite independently. With both libraries practical expediency rather than any theoretical factors has dominated.

Directories
CBL has a subject classification for British Isles and international directories which allocates numbers from 00 to 99 without further extension. (1)

Outline
 0 General production and manufactures
 1 Chemical industries
 2 Fabrics
 3 Engineering, building, planning and property
 4 Service industries, public utilities
 5 Transport and communications
 6 Distribution of goods and ideas
 7 Finance, commercial administration and law
 8 Public life
 9 Other activities
Chemical industries is subdivided as follows
 10 Chemical industries in general
 11 Pharmacy
 12 Rubber
 13 Plastics

14 Metals
15 Pottery and glass
16 Soap and other surface finishes
17 Other chemical products
18 Waste trades

Overseas directories are arranged by marketing areas in the following order which is largely dictated by the lay-out of the library

1 Australasia, Oceania
2 North America
3 Western Europe generally
4 EEC countries
5 EFTA countries
6 Other Western European countries
7 Eastern Europe
8 Middle East
9 Far East
10 Africa
11 Latin America
12 Caribbean

Within these areas, countries are arranged alphabetically and further subdivided by the subject classification.

MCL arranges general directories in Dewey order of geographical area covered (with slight modifications for trade areas like the EC) but, instead of Dewey notation, uses an arbitrary three digit and letter through numbering. No directory has a unique number. This numbering continues with subject directories, whether British or overseas, which are arranged in alphabetical order of subject. The alphabetisation is not necessarily by specific subject. 'Board' and 'concrete' directories are put with 'building', 'paint manufacturing' and 'perfumery' with 'chemicals' but 'plastics' is treated separately. This grouping of subjects into trade areas might seem confusing but, if the alphabetisation is made clear by shelf guides, the public always appear to understand an alphabetical arrangement, with all its defects, better than a logical classification. Directories are listed on a visible index under geographical or national headings; there is no listing under subjects but merely a reference to the relevant directory stand number.

The advantage of the CBL scheme is that all national directories, regardless of subject, can be seen together and it is easy to lead on from say a German general trades directory to a more specialised one. In contrast, the MCL scheme puts all subject directories together, regardless of country of origin, and it easy to lead on from say a European textile directory to a French textile directory.

Periodicals

CBL uses the same arrangement for periodicals as directories except that there is no trade sub-division of overseas countries. MCL uses approximate Dewey order for displayed periodicals with fixed location and each display stand allocated a particular subject and running number. A visible index lists periodicals alphabetically by title and country with a reference to the number of the relevant display stand. In the periodical stack, arrangement is alphabetical by title in two separate sequences—'binding' and 'non-binding'.

Market product and industry data

Material, other than directories and periodicals, on specific overseas countries is arranged at the CBL in a separate sequence with a prefix A followed by the relevant Dewey geographical sub-division. This would include statistical handbooks, central bank reports, geographical and economic studies, market surveys and reports on products and industries. International coverage of marketing and economic matters is in this sequence but material relating to a particular product or industry, with either international or British coverage, is allocated to a separate sequence prefixed B followed by the appropriate Dewey number without the decimal point. Thus books, pamphlets and series dealing with the aircraft industry, British or international, would be classed at B62913 whilst those on the German aircraft industry at A43. This follows the same principle as the arrangement of directories, where the geographical factor is dominant over subject content.

At the MCL, there is a considerable difference in approach. This type of material is separated into three distinct groups—statistics, vertical file and Dewey sequence.

Statistics (2)

As a rough guide, statistical publications are taken to be those in which the text consists of more numerals than letters. They are arranged in a separate sequence in the following classified

50

arrangement with a prefix 'S'.

000–099 General guides, weights and measures, bibliographies
100–249 United Kingdom   Arranged by subject
250–399 International
400–499 Europe
500–599 Asia   Subdivided alphabetically
600–699 Africa   by country
700–799 North America
800–899 South America
900–999 Australasia
An example of subject arrangement is
360 industries—international
361 furniture
362 building and housing
364 paper
365 chemicals
366 leather, hides
367 textiles, clothing
368 engineering

Thus UK textile statistics—S217; international textile statistics—S367; US textile statistics—S790. Again the geographical factor is dominant. Statistical publications are entered on a strip index, alphabetically by subject, with a separate sequence alphabetically by country. Items of statistical importance in other kinds of material such as periodicals, directories and the vertical file are also entered on this index.

Vertical file (3) (4)
Pamphlet material, clippings, cyclostyled pages and certain miscellaneous items are arranged in a vertical file under about a thousand headings which fall into the following main groups
     Countries—continents, multinational groupings followed by individual countries arranged alphabetically
     Commercial and economic subjects—these include advertising, automation, employment, finance, management, taxation, trade, all with further subdivisions
     Commodities and industries—main topics arranged alphabetically, then further subdivided
     Transport and communications

General eg, appointments, associations, charities, coming events, defence, education

The alphabetico-classed arrangement of the four non-geographical groups is illustrated in the following example

Commodities and Industries
  Food and agriculture
    —agriculture
    —food
      —convenience foods
    —products and crops
      —beverages
        —beer
        —cocoa
        —coffee
        —tea
        —wines and spirits
      —bread and confectionery
      —cereals and grains
      —dairy products
      —eggs and poultry

There is a dictionary index of specific headings available. The arrangement in each drawer is fairly obvious as full length strip headings are used for every file and the schedule is easily apparent. The system is very flexible; subjects are continuously being altered, combined or divided. The previous book classification arrangement was found to be too difficult to work, slow in use and subjects were not easily accepted (eg, the Dewey number for 'coming events', 'appointments' or 'Zaire' are not readily apparent).

Dewey sequence
Both CBL and MCL have Dewey book shelf sequences for such subjects as law and management although in MCL inclusion in this sequence is dictated by the physical form of material, ie, books and pamphlets which are too large to be accommodated in the vertical file.

A number of classification schemes have been devised to cover the literature of business; that used at the London Graduate School of Business Studies is the most notable. (5)

Other sequences

The following are examples of other separate sequences

Dictionaries—alphabetical by language

Gazetteers—alphabetical by country

Company services—alphabetical by the form of company name used by the service. Extel use a three letter filing code which may not correspond to the alphabetisation used generally in the library.

Company reports—alphabetically by name of company omitting initials in personal names. (The Company Registry includes these initials in the official list of companies and thus A B Smith Ltd is entered under A).

Timetables—alphabetically by country. UK local bus timetables are often arranged geographically.

Official guides—alphabetically by county and town.

Maps—alphabetically by continent and country, then by scale.

Records

Particularly where there is a central reference catalogue, a conventional catalogue is largely unnecessary in a business library. Strip indexes, published bibliographies and staff information files are more efficient substitutes, as well as being more economic. Sufficient information can be entered on a strip for most users. For example, with maps, the country, scale and location are sufficient. On the few occasions when an inquirer needs details of the cartographer and dates of survey, it is more efficient for him to consult the actual sheets than for the staff to record little used information.

As has been said, permanently retained material will be entered in the central reference catalogue in the usual way. It will be kept in the business library probably only for a year or two whilst it has business interest and then transferred to another department. There does not seem any need to catalogue other material such as overseas telephone directories, although some libraries make entries for such serial items with the cards marked 'Current copy in business library'. It is not always easy to decide when first received whether a particular item is worth permanent preservation and the opportunity should be taken of making a second judgement, with perhaps more perspective, when it is about to be discarded. One generation's rubbish can be another generation's treasure trove and there are many examples of material, once available in business libraries and not now preserved in any library, which would be of immense interest to modern research workers.

Each catalogued item is centrally shelf listed and allocated a unique call number which remains the same regardless of the department in which it may be located at any time. The business library will have a parallel shelf list in order of the book classification scheme for all catalogued items on its stock. If the item is in one of the groups which has a special arrangement, then there will be a reference from the entry in this shelf list to the special number eg, 338.4766 Ch 4 Chemical industry statistics handbook 1973 S210. Separate shelf lists must also be maintained for each of the main special groups in the order of that group for the purpose of allocating a number, providing the date of the edition held and stock-taking. In the directory shelf-list, for example, only a small proportion of the items will be catalogued and there will be a reference in the entry for each of these back to the unique call number eg, DS 714E *Bureau Veritas Registre* 1973 387.2 B12. A directory which is permanently filed will carry the call number on the back of the title-page but, whilst located in the business library, will have the directory stand number on its spine. If it is requested in another department by someone using the central catalogue, its location is found to be the business library from the central shelf-register and its directory stand number from the main business library shelf-list. On the other hand, if a reader in the business library wanted to know the retrospective holdings of a directory currently displayed, then the call number can be obtained from the directory itself or the directory shelf list and then reference can be made to the central shelf register where the holdings are recorded. As such a large proportion of the business library stock is made up of annuals, serials and other continuations the maintenance of these shelf-lists is not as difficult as it may seem.

The map shelf list is a little more complex because individual sheets in a series may be received over a period of many years. In the case of 1:10,000 maps, each shelf list page consists of the 100 km lettered grid square subdivided into 100 squares each quartered to represent a sheet and corresponding to the numbering of the national grid. When a sheet is received the appropriate square is struck through.

Card indexes

For pamphlet material in the vertical file, books in the Dewey

54

sequence and certain statistical publications with distinctive titles, a staff card index is maintained with entries made on pragmatic rather than theoretical principles (eg, reports would be entered under their popular names used by the press, *UK balance of payments* would have an entry under 'pink').

Staff compiled indexes are the touchstone of a business service and would probably include the following sequences: 1 general information; 2 local companies; 3 trade names (purchased from the patent office); 4 local buildings; 5 districts in the area covered by the electoral register collection; 6 streets; 7 town plans; 8 official guides; 9 retail prices; 10 sources of prices; 11 periodical binding.

Chapter 4

Special considerations of company libraries

Alan Armstrong

Executives who bear the responsibility for the present profitability and future direction of their companies must make their decisions on the best information available. This information is generated by other employees—planners, accountants, computer staff. In this process the business library plays a role. Its significance is dependent upon the personality of the librarian, but his place in the management team is purely optional. If the businessman falls sick he must go to a doctor, similarly to a dentist or analyst; no businessman has to go to a librarian or information officer for business information. If a businessman uses a company library, it will be only one of many interrelated and complex sources he uses. The role of the librarian in industry is therefore unconventional when compared with librarians in universities or local government where the 'optional' library is unthinkable.

There are very few 'subject' company libraries, unlike the subject libraries of university faculties. The work of the business librarian must reflect at all times the prevailing activities and corporate ambitions of the company. The service is geared to corporate needs, mission orientated and operates in an atmosphere where change is progress. User needs may demand unconventional practices which are unacceptable in the conventional library.

Why does a company need a business library?
Every day more and more external influences bear upon decisions

taken inside companies. Businessmen have to keep up with these changes, and be respectful of them, whether they are market changes, legislative changes or fashion changes. Hard pressed executives in every industry keep pace with all the external factors in many different ways. Hopes that computers would assist executives with the torrent of outside information, as they have with internal data, have largely proved illusory. The time honoured methods of acquiring information prevail, but the volume needed and received far exceeds the capacity of executives to absorb it. Inadequate and inaccessible information is the executives' biggest timewaster.

Today the volume of the flow of important information is such that more and more companies are adding business libraries to their more traditional technical libraries. (The term business library is used here also to mean and encompass company information centres, economic intelligence departments, commercial libraries; and by business librarian is also meant information officers, managers of economic intelligence units and any other fancy titles which mean business librarian.)

Business libraries exist to monitor the twenty four hour a day flow of business information; the relevant is separated from the unnecessary, then indexed and stored. Important information is passed to executives either regularly to a known interest, or later on demand. The information is deliberately stored for, and fed to, those executives whose daily decisions must either make money, or save money for their company.

For the last five years, the executive and the business librarian have been moving closer together. The executive must now have fast daily access to external information and business librarians as a profession have been building the network to provide it. The relationship between the executive and the business librarian has never been better, but equally it has never been easy. To a businessman who traditionally obtained facts from business contacts and trade associations, by visiting clients, or by overseas trade missions, the library at first seemed incongruous. He had been brought up on the educational libraries at school, college, university and even professional institution. With his family he was able to enjoy the educational and recreational facilities of his local public library.

It has taken a long time to convince the businessman that the company library is not for education or recreation—but purely for exploitation. A new generation of more extrovert librarians is showing that business libraries exist to exploit all published information, using sophisticated methods, and that they are providing this information, not in a quiet and leisurely way, but while you wait. This exploitation of published data is the business librarian's output. The output from the library is information. This output—this information—is what the company needs and demands. It does not want the books, the catalogues, the shelving, or the librarian—unless she is pretty. It simply wants the output—the information.

The business librarian achieves this in two ways, first by using the material and stock of the library, that is the directories, the timetables, the microfilm, computer printout, journals, reports, files, newspapers, press cuttings, yearbooks, maps and even encyclopaedias. The second way is by going outside the library to external and specialist sources of information. The result in both cases is output—information. The executive does not care where it is from as long as it is regarded as accurate information from an accurate source. The ability to provide accurate information quickly demonstrates the business librarian as an equal specialist, inside the management team, alongside other professional businessmen generating internal information by computer or perhaps monitoring information on internal performance as an accountant. Thus the business librarian will spend more time out of the office making and maintaining external contacts than he will spend on precision cataloguing.

The duties of a business librarian
Unlike the academic or public librarian who serves all comers, the company often employs a librarian to serve a limited number of employees, perhaps at one location, or even in one department. An unpalatable task for the young librarian in industry is to deny service to many employees. The library will exist for a particular purpose, usually to provide information to a planning, sales, legal or marketing department, or a combination of departments. From one of these departments the librarian receives his budget; whoever thus sponsors the library will expect complete support and undiluted effort. The business librarian must keep the ambitions of the company and that department continually in mind. To attempt to run a 'public' library for employees is to court disaster.

Within the department or location, the librarian's role is professionally agressive. The present commercial and legislative information explosion is creating an impossible chore for the businessman. Not only does he expect instant information from the specialist, but he expects to lodge a 'watching brief' with the librarian, so that he can have the press regularly monitored to his own stated interests. The librarian who achieves this at executive level proves himself to be a real asset, and his library rated as a 'performance department'. The passive librarian who waits for the businessman to come will wait—and wait.

It is not easy for a young librarian to walk into a senior executive's office and sell the professional ability and services of the library. It can be achieved by a simple formula. Produce a summary of the week's published news as it affects your company. Include news of clients and competitors and better still prospective clients and competitors; include market conditions, summaries of new legislation, then distribute it by agreement to key executives. This not only saves them from conscientious reading, but is itself a tangible weekly output of your service. Soon recipients will come to you to ask for more information on a topic you covered; at that point provide the information and sell your services. The executive's secretary is your ally—supply her with timetables, *Who's who*, addresses, atlases, dictionaries, until she can tell her boss what you are capable of.

The librarian's place in the company structure
Every company group wants to report to the managing director or president. Public relations and advertising men want to, so do planners, administrators, lawyers, accountants. In practice there has to be a corporate tree and in that tree the library will find its level according to its purpose and personality.

The first aim is to report to a policy maker, someone who is setting the pace at which the company moves. Aim to attach your service to a thruster, not a sleeper. If as so often happens the library manager is a coronary gentleman over 60, your aim should be to move onto someone else's budget. This is desirable but highly difficult. The higher up the tree, the better are the budgets and the less drastic the cutbacks. After all you are probably a graduate, professionally qualified, a specialist and quite possibly a little better read than some other employees. Do not let yourself be treated as a messenger, photocopier or typist; this will impair the efficiency and purpose of the appointment. You should have access to part time clerical and secretarial assistance. Be one of the team—as an equal. Display your skills confidently and you will earn the respect of your professional colleagues as an information specialist, just as you may admire their skills as accountants and lawyers. The place of the library in the structure of the company depends on two factors—your efficiency and your personality. One without the other is insufficient to raise the library off the bottom of the corporate tree.

Staffing

Librarians and accountants, administrators, planners are non-productive staff (producing no goods or services to sell), thus falling into a category of employee that no company enjoys. An efficient company employs as few non-productive staff as possible. Therefore no business library should be bigger than required to provide the service. Empire builders are unwelcome. Keep staff to a minimum and never recruit 'cataloguers', always recruit to an 'active' post, where justification can be displayed by some tangible new service. Beware of the demarcation between non-professional, librarian and information scientist; disregard the label and choose the best candidate.

Stock

The stock carried in-house must be balanced against what is freely available by phone, from external sources. Your company will be in membership of professional bodies, either corporately or through individual employees. These will give access to specialised and free information services. Use them instead of building up your own stock. Other special libraries will carry useful stock to which you have access. In turn you will maintain highly specialised publications, peculiar to the interests of the company, so be prepared to lend or give information which is published, in the same way as you often seek it from others. A basic reference stock in-house is an essential foundation to good service and will include directories, dictionaries, timetables, atlases, handbooks, guidebooks, just as in any reference library. To these will be added the 'speciality' publications of your industry.

Remember the external commercial subscription services too, where you can buy access to published information. The modern library achieves economies by using many such services instead of building up data of peripheral or transitory interest.

The future

If the new generation of business librarians demonstrate ability to relieve the executive's information burden by orderly monitoring, storing, retrieving and advising of important data, they will hold a secure place supporting the company's policy makers. Top management needs accurate information on which to base its daily decisions which must make money or save money, now or in the future.

Perhaps it is the fast pace of change, or the presumed insecurity of commercial life which deters so many librarians from entering this type of library. Less than 2% of British library school leavers enter company libraries; the majority of such units are run by non-librarian staff. The opportunity for the trained librarian is limitless and promotion is fast. It is one type of library where humour exceeds politics. The challenge of participating with a major contribution to an industrial or commercial management team awaits any librarian with enthusiasm, personality and efficiency.

Chapter 5

Directories and company information sources

George P Henderson

1 The importance of directories

The human race is always on the move—people, business firms, government departments, even major industrial enterprises. Moreover, human progress depends on the exploitation of new ideas—ideas which require not only the application of science and technology for their development but also the discovery of new sources of supply for materials, new sources of advice and ideas for their marketing, new services for their distribution and new customers in new markets for their commercial success. It is in the context of a changing world which is constantly seeking to make new contacts that the true importance of directories can be seen as a vital aid to communication. Yet directories are probably the least known, least understood and least fully exploited types of reference work.

Most people—and in fact many librarians—would be hard put to it to name one directory other than the telephone book; that even businessmen lack full appreciation and knowledge of directories has been demonstrated again and again by the gullibility with which they succumb to the tricks of bogus directory operators (see para 8 below). It is therefore necessary to begin this chapter with some explanation of the factors governing the compilation and publication of directories, factors which also determine the existence or absence of published directory information of various kinds.

The majority of legitimate directories belong to either of two categories: 1) those produced as a commercial venture and available through normal trade channels and 2) those forming part of the administrative or promotional publications of a society, institution or government department and available either through the book trade, or direct from the organisation concerned, or distributed to selected recipients. As the latter category is generally less exposed to economic factors, the following remarks apply mainly to category 1).

2 Directory compilation and publication

Directory compilation falls naturally into three main processes: 1) assembly of a base list 2) elaboration and checking by postal or personal canvass 3) editing and indexing.

The base list in many cases is the previous edition of the directory; an entirely new directory may require the collation of any existing lists, the building up of a list from a multiplicity of sources, the street-by-street and town-by-town listing of units within a district or region, or a mixture of all three. Postal checking requires a carefully designed questionnaire, possibly with a cutting of the previous edition's entry or a suggested wording for a new entry; personal canvassing, to be effective, requires individuals with patience, tact and considerable physical endurance. Editing and indexing involve problems of alphabetisation and heading-selection varying from one directory to another, often in accordance with the requirements of the type of user for which it is intended.

All the above processes are labour-intensive and therefore expensive; moreover the printing of directories requires high standards of accuracy and successive editions often require either resetting or extensive alterations to standing type. Consequently commercial publishers of directories are constantly seeking methods by which to supplement the revenue obtained from sale of copies. Many favour the practice whereby any firm within the scope (geographical and industrial) of a directory is entitled to free entry of, for example, its name, address, telephone number and brief business description in the A–Z listing and free entries of its name and postal address in up to three entries in the 'classified trades' listing; a firm that wishes to appear in bold type, or to have additional information printed in its entries, or to be listed under each of its fifty seven different products, may do so on payment according to a set scale of charges. This practice is generally understood and appreciated by business, and a number of our older and most valuable directories (eg, *Kelly's Post Office London directory*) are able to appear at remarkably low prices thanks to the revenue so obtained.

Naturally the converse applies; the structure and trading characteristics of certain industries and trades are such that no amount of publishing ingenuity can make a directory viable. And the city directories of many of our large towns have been driven out of existence by a combination of economic factors which have made them impossible to publish without heavy loss. Hence the many and often surprising gaps which the librarian must be ready to explain to sceptical enquirers—eg, no city directories of Leeds, Nottingham, Plymouth—no national trade directories of hatters, do-it-yourself shops, drapers or photographic studios.

There are, of course, a number of directory publishers, producing valuable works of reference, who for good reasons prefer not to include 'paid matter' or to accept advertisements; the purchaser must recognise the fact that the prices of such unsubsidised directories may be relatively higher.

3 Selection and acquisition

Directories are the bedrock upon which the stock of any business library must be built. Many businessmen can succeed without studying economics or management, without giving a thought to market research or even research and development, but very few businesses can function without having to find new customers, new sources of supply, etc. It is therefore essential to the development of a business library to have a clear policy for building up an effective directory stock.

Directories are relatively expensive and rapidly become out of date. Considerable skill is necessary therefore to avoid two frustrating possibilities—1) too small a stock, from which the business users never find the answer they need, and therefore give up using the library, or 2) too large a stock acquired at great expense, but underused because the business public in the library's catchment area needs time to become accustomed to the idea of using its resources. The ideal is to keep slightly ahead of demand, so that the business user is always agreeably surprised to find that the library has recently obtained a directory he needs, in anticipation of his demand.

The options open to the librarian with a limited book fund are—1) to acquire every edition of a carefully selected small stock of directories, or 2) to cover a wider range by purchasing an edition of each directory every two, three or four years. Probably the best solution is a blend of both possibilities, purchasing every edition of the most heavily used items and relegating others to less frequent acquisition. Occasionally it is necessary to decide between two or more equally valuable directories of the same industry (for many years there have been two closely similar directories of the paper trade); almost certainly a business user will complain, whichever is chosen, and the opportunity thus occurs to obtain his expert advice in readiness for the next editions.

A basic stock for the business library in the UK can be built from the following elements:

1) a complete set of A–Z and cfd telephone directories of the UK, Eire and Channel Islands,

2) UK telex directory,

3) *Kelly's Post Office London directory* and street directories (where they exist) of other major cities,

4) general commercial and industrial directories, particularly: *Kompass UK; Kelly's Manufacturers and merchants directory;* D & B *Key British enterprises;* D & B *British middle market directory; Sell's directory,*

5) general financial yearbooks, particularly: *Stock Exchange official year book; Jane's Major companies of Europe,*

6) general government and local government directories, particularly: *Civil Service year book; Municipal year book,*

7) general directories of associations and organisations, particularly: *Directory of British associations; Councils, committees and boards,*

8) general directories of people, particularly: *Who's who; Kelly's handbook; Directory of directors,*

9) specialised directories of major industries, eg: *Chemical industry directory; Skinner's British textile register; Electrical & electronic trades directory; Iron and steel works of the world; Stores, shops, supermarkets retail directory,*

10) directories or membership lists of the professions, eg: *Law list; Medical directory; RIBA directory,*

11) coverage in depth of directories germane to any local industries, with special emphasis on directories of their markets, if identifiable,

12) overseas directories (see para 6 below).

The business librarian should be aware of the many opportunities to acquire directory material free of charge; some

chambers of commerce and many trade associations and professional organisations are only too glad to supply copies of their
directories or membership lists to libraries that will use them effectively.

4 Arrangement and control of stock

Like many other elements of library stock, directories can either be
brought together as a special form, or be dispersed among other material. Certain libraries may find it advantageous to shelve *Kelly's directory of Norwich* among the topographical works at 914.261, or to
place the *Law list* alongside *Halsbury* and *Stone's justice's manual*.
But for the business library it is essential to concentrate current directories into a directory unit; further, it is often desirable that the directory stock should attract works such as technical yearbooks which
include 'buyers guides' or lists of trade names, special directory
issues of trade periodicals, catalogues of trade fairs and exhibitions,
etc.

Regarding shelf arrangement of directories, there is a primary
practical distinction between local directories and special-subject directories. The enquirer who wishes to check an address in, say, Norwich, will need to try first *Kelly's directory of Norwich* or the
telephone directory, or perhaps the voters list for Norwich. By
reason of their special arrangement and indexing it is always best to
keep telephone directories together in a single sequence. City and
town directories shelved in A–Z order present the minimum problem
of access for the man in the street; Dewey or similar regional arrangements can create an unnecessary obstruction to quick-reference use.

The dominant factor in determining the shelf arrangement of
specialised directories is the fact that a large proportion of enquiries
involve the use of all available directories in a broad subject group.
For example the identification of the manufacturer of a specific
brand of paint may require resort to a dozen or more directories
covering the whole range of activities from public works to plumbing. There is therefore a *prima facie* advantage in arranging specialised directories under fairly broad headings. This concept was put
into practical form in Guildhall Library's Commercial Reference
Room in 1950 when a special classification was devised, using a two-
digit notation from 00–99, the following being a typical sequence:

02 Agriculture

03 Fisheries

04 Food
05 Drink
06 Tobacco

The classification soon proved to have a number of advantages, some of them unexpected: a) it is simple to memorise, b) two figures can be applied to the spines of most directories in sufficiently bold type to enable misplaced items to be readily spotted, c) it was easy to extend its use to classify specialised directories of overseas countries, d) it facilitated the provision of readily identifiable box-locations for flimsy material (see below).

The scheme has since been adopted by other business libraries, notably Birmingham; copies can be obtained from the City Business Library.

Directories come in a great variety of shapes and sizes, and in a heavily used stock 'pamphlet' material (often containing more significant lists than the 'heavies') can easily become torn or lost. This problem can be overcome by housing flimsy or small items in boxes shelved in the main run of directories and clearly marked with the class or group of classes contained in them.

In the arrangement and display of directories it is unfortunately necessary to bear in mind the very real possibility of theft. Every directory represents a list of business prospects for somebody, and all too often the temptation to help oneself proves irresistible; this can be particularly damaging when the item removed is a key item and out of print. The directories most likely to be stolen vary from one library to another and can only be identified by experience; but one thing is certain—if a directory is stolen, its replacement and successive editions will continue to be stolen. The remedy lies in the exercise of specific control over the directories known to be bad risks; this may take the form of keeping such directories at the enquiry desk, or the use of an electronic monitoring service such as the one recently installed in the City Business Library, London. If the former practice is adopted it is an advantage to provide marker blocks on the shelf indicating eg, *Stores, shops, supermarkets retail directory*—please apply at desk.

The nuisance of theft can to some extent be mitigated by retaining previous editions of directories and making them available for loan. Particularly when the current edition is unobtainable through being out of print the loan copy can provide the would-be purchaser with access to *an* edition, albeit a year or two out of date, for use in his office for a few weeks; and if the current edition is stolen and proves irreplaceable then the loan copy can be brought back into service until the appearance of the next edition.

5 Types of directory enquiries

Directories can be used to answer three main types of enquiries—location, identification and elaboration.

i *Location*

The simplest examples in this category are questions such as 'We know that Tweedle and Dee are a Liverpool firm—what is their street address?', which can be answered without hesitation from such sources as the Liverpool telephone directory. If however, the question is simply 'Where can we find Bray and Barker Ltd?' the problem is less easy; if the enquirer can recall that they are paint manufacturers or shipping agents or meat wholesalers the search can be narrowed to relevant specialised directories; but failing that the procedure is first to try the longest available alphabetical lists of companies—*Kelly's manufacturers & merchants, Kompass, Key British enterprises, Rylands directory* etc, in the hope that the concern is large enough to be listed; failing which a steady search through all sixty areas of the telephone directory may be the only alternative to referring the enquirer to Companies House. Enquiries do occasionally require the location of an enterprise of which the country of domicile is not known; if it has a suffix (such as GmbH or SpA) the special table provided in *European Companies* (see para 10) will narrow the search down to the countries using such suffixes in Europe; the business librarian will quickly learn to spot other clues such as Pty or Pvt indicating Australian or South African or Rhodesian private companies; but if the suffix is SA—used universally in French and Spanish speaking countries—or if there is *no* suffix, the search may be very wide indeed.

ii *Identification*

This is a much broader category, including questions as simple as:

'Who is headmaster of Eton?' or 'Who occupies 73 Portland Place, London W1?' and relatively complex ones such as: 'Who makes garden tools bearing the brand-name "Hortool"?' 'Which are the ten largest aluminium products manufacturers in Canada?' 'Of which companies is Kurt Schumacher a director?' 'Which shipping lines operate between Rotterdam and Dakar?'

Questions of this type often require deeper knowledge of the resources of a directory stock than do 'location' enquiries; reference to the 'trade names' heading in the index to *Current British directories* will also demonstrate the fact that many items not normally regarded as directories will have to be consulted in trade mark and trade name enquiries, and the same applies to many other specialised types of identification query. By bringing together information about a great deal of fringe directory material, and by analysing and indexing many of the little-known resources embedded in specialised directories, *CBD* takes the searcher far along the road to a solution of identification enquiries; but no index or bibliography can be an adequate substitute for experience, ingenuity and often sheer intuition in handling these enquiries.

iii *Elaboration of data*
By elaboration of data is meant the type of enquiry beginning 'We want to find as much as possible about Mr X, Company Y or Organisation Z'. Often the enquiry can be narrowed down to finding if Mr X is married, if Company Y has an agent in Sweden or if organisation Z holds an annual conference, details which can be readily obtained from entries in *Who's who, Kompass* or *Directory of British associations*. But if extensive information is required, the chances are high that conventional directory resources may soon be exhausted, and it will be necessary to resort to investors' services, newspaper or trade press files, collections of annual reports, trade catalogues etc. (see para 7 below)

iv *Company relationships enquiries*
One particularly important type of 'elaboration' enquiry deserves special mention: the 'who owns whom' question. The enlargement of the EEC has given stimulus to the already considerable activity leading to mergers, take-overs and other forms of company linkage, especially across frontiers. A great many company relationship enquiries can be answered expeditiously from the *Who owns whom* series published by O W Roskill, or from the company affiliation tables in the *Stock Exchange official yearbook* and *Key British enterprises*; but if not, or if the enquirer needs more detailed or extensive information about the nature of the relationship, then the answer will have to be sought elsewhere. Among the sources to be tried are:

70

a) the *Directory of directors* and other indexes to directors, in the hope of finding names common to both companies; b) the consolidated indexes to financial yearbooks and investors' services, which normally include the subsidiaries of the quoted companies they describe; c) directories—such as the *Anglo-American trade directory*—issued by international chambers of commerce, which can frequently establish the existence of commercial relationships, however tenuous, between companies in one country and another; d) press indexes and abstracts (see para 7v), in the hope of finding reports, rumours or comments, especially when a take-over has been bruited but not finalised.

There are, of course, a number of overseas sources for company relationships, notable examples being *Les Liaisons financières* (France) and *Konzerne in Schaubildern* (Germany); the latter is unique in presenting the information in the form of diagrams not unlike family trees.

6 Overseas directories

Many business houses have their own resources for answering domestic directory enquiries, but for overseas information have to rely on the business library not only for the directories themselves but for assistance in their use. Consequently, by their very nature, overseas directory enquiries are the most exciting and rewarding of business library activities. The selection, acquisition, maintenance and exploitation of a stock of overseas directories present special problems and require a number of special skills. A complete description of overseas directory work would require a separate chapter; the following notes may serve to provide some guidance:

i *Selection*

For almost every country the telephone directories comprise an inexpensive, easily acquired, reliable and comprehensible basic stock; but beware of attempting 'blanket coverage'—*all* Finland or *all* Canada or *all* Spain will contain many areas which will remain unused for decades, and *all* USA will immobilise the library completely! An intelligent selection of capital and other big cities will provide a stock from which a high proportion of 'location' enquiries can be answered.

But telephone directories have limited application—particularly where company or product information is required. Many countries have a well established general commercial directory which brings together in one work a variety of information designed to serve the needs of the businessman in each country. A good example is *Kraks vejviser* (Denmark) which includes information on government departments, trade associations etc; a complete alphabetical register of businesses with appropriate data; a classified trades directory, and alphabetical and streets directories of Copenhagen.

The Kompass series provides examples of industrial directories of a particularly important type—those which include more information about individual enterprises than simply name and address. Another notable directory in this class is *Handbuch der Grossunternehmen*, which gives directors' names, production programme, turnover, number of employees and other basic information on 22,000 major German companies. For the major industrial countries the field of selection opens out at this point to a wide range of specialised directories of all kinds, and most libraries find it necessary to limit their acquisitions to those which have some relevance for their local industries or pattern of enquiries.

In the building of overseas directory stocks there is much scope for cooperation between business libraries in the same area.

ii *Acquisition*
Overseas telephone and telex directories are easily obtainable through the post office. Certain commercial directory publishers have agencies established in the UK and other countries (eg, *ABC der Deutschen Wirtschaft*—Dirag Ltd, Birmingham); all the Kompass series are available from the Kompass office at Croydon. For others the choice lies between direct purchase, the book trade, or specialist agencies; of the latter, BAS Overseas Publications Ltd has specialised for many years in supplying foreign directories to British libraries, and provides an efficient and reliable service. In ordering overseas directories two important factors should be borne in mind: 1) certain directories may be unexpectedly expensive by comparison with similar British works—it is always advisable to verify the price before placing a firm order; 2) many important directories go out of print within a few weeks of publication, and this possibility should be constantly borne in mind when stock-building.

iii *Handling overseas directory enquiries*
The following points are of vital importance:

72

1) A considerable number of specialised directories produced in the UK are international in scope; the best of them often provide more accurate and easily accessible information than do indigenous sources of the subject-country of the enquiry.

2) Any librarian committed to handling overseas directories should acquire familiarity with certain basic terms in the major languages eg: Branchenverzeichnis; Elenco; Vejviser; Matrikel; Årbog; Leverantörregister; Medlemsfortegnelser; Yrkesregister.

3) Even more important, the numerous variations in alphabetical practices between one country and another must be borne in mind; examples are the position of modified vowels ä, ø, å, etc, in Scandinavian languages and German, the special position of ch in Spanish etc; (see the notes on alphabetisation given under country in *Current European directories* and *European companies*.)

4) Directories are generally produced to serve the needs of the 'home' user, and anyone else must be prepared to use them with this in mind. Street addresses, for example, are drastically abbreviated particularly in American and Spanish telephone directories, and the user would be well advised not to address mail using only the abbreviated form given, eg: 1682 Hk Frwy S; Gral Mol 82; 4° F Av Mg Tom; Kirkev 52 pa K.

7 Other sources of information about business enterprises

As already indicated in paragraph 5(iii), directories can only satisfy a relatively small proportion of enquiries that call for elaboration of information about specific companies or other forms of business enterprise. This section discusses major categories of information sources to which the business enquirer may resort.

i *Statutory information*—ie, the documents which a limited company must, by law, lodge with the Registrar of Companies (in GB) or other appropriate authorities.

Under British law the file of every limited company contains, *inter alia*, the company's Memorandum and Articles of Association, the address of its registered office, the names and addresses of its directors, the list of shareholders, and an annual return which must include the latest balance sheet and profit & loss account; this file is available for inspection by personal applicants at Companies House on payment of a nominal fee.

There is also a register of business names (also at Companies House) with which particulars of any form of business operating under a 'business name' must be lodged.

Comparable public access to official records of business enterprises is provided in other countries; a notable difference outside the UK is that either the full text or summaries of all documents are published in an official government gazette; a further difference is that in several countries, eg, France, *all* forms of business enterprises—even individual traders—must be inscribed in the Registre du Commerce.

For details of official registers, and the facilities that they provide for public access to their records, see *European companies* and *Current African directories*.

ii *Investors' services*

Voluminous documentation on 'quoted' companies—ie, those whose shares are admitted for quotation on the Stock Exchange—is provided in various services intended primarily for the investor and the financial market generally.

Two closely similar services, Extel and Moodies, each provide subscribers with a series of 'cards' relating to c 5,000 British quoted companies; each card contains: history and description of the company; names of directors and secretary; capital history and structure; dividend and yield records; extensive tabulated analyses of its balance sheets and profit and loss accounts over a period of years; various ratios which enable its progress to be assessed; significant points from the latest company meeting. Subscribers receive up-dated information on replacement cards distributed daily or weekly.

Besides the two services mentioned above, Extel also offers an 'Unquoted companies' service, giving similar details for 1,500 major private companies.

Numerous other card or loose-leaf services covering for example major European companies (*Extel European companies service*, and *Informations internationales*), German companies (*Das Spezial-Archiv der Deutschen Wirtschaft*), French companies (*Les notices SEF/DAFSA*) are described in *European companies*. Services covering Australia, Canada and South Africa are available from Moodies Services Ltd, London.

iii *Credit information services*

Public libraries are occasionally asked if they have *Bradstreet's Register* or *Seyd*'s; the answer must invariably be 'No', because these registers are confidential documents issued only to subscribers to Dun and Bradstreet's credit reporting service. There are several such services operating in each major country, of which quite a few have world-wide reporting networks; they undertake to provide their subscribers with reports containing, *inter alia*, an assessment of the subject enterprise's ability to pay; an adverse credit rating, if communicated to a third party, may constitute a libel—hence the need for confidentiality. Certain agencies, of which Dun and Bradstreet is one, assemble ratings and other data into printed registers which subscriber companies can lease for constant reference in their credit-control departments. These registers constitute a source of much information not readily available from published directories, but they are *only* accessible to business subscribers.

iv *Company reports*

A valuable picture of any major company can be obtained from its own published report, which is often designed—and illustrated—in order to project the 'image' of the company among its shareholders and potential shareholders.

The City Business Library now has a collection of reports of many thousands of British companies and foreign companies; and several other public commercial libraries have stocks of reports, particularly of companies in their own regions. There can be no doubt that business library users will always welcome and refer to company reports if provided; but the formation of a collection does raise special problems of selection, acquisition, storage and discarding upon which the librarian should seek advice from someone who has already a collection in being.

v *Financial and trade press*

Apart from investors' services, a great deal of recent news about companies is contained in newspapers and trade periodicals. To tap these resources fully it is necessary either to maintain a special index or an extensive news clipping file, or to use published indexes and abstracting services. *Research index*, published fortnightly, indexes, both by subject and by company names, financial news appearing in some 150 journals; *McCarthy information services* go further, providing photocopies of significant news and comment on all British quoted and major unquoted, companies; on a wider scale, services such as *F and S Index international, Chemical market abstracts* and

Middle East economic digest provide leads to important items of company news in various parts of the world.

8 Fraudulent directories

As mentioned earlier, the business community has been plagued for many years by fraudulent operators who sell entries or advertisements in non-existent or worthless directories. The Unsolicited Goods and Services Act 1971 curbed some of the worst offenders, but rackets continue and are likely to emerge in other forms. The UK is not the only country to be plagued with bogus directories, and many operate on an international scale; the problem of combatting them was the major cause which led to the formation in 1968 of the European Association of Directory Publishers. Subsequently in 1970 the UK members of the European Association formed the Association of British Directory Publishers, which has two principal aims: 1) to protect the public from the activities of fraudulent directory promoters; and 2) by mutual discussion of technical problems to provide the nation with more efficient directories.

The businessman who has reason to be suspicious of a document emanating from a directory publisher may seek guidance from the public library. It is not difficult to recognise the bogus proposition—the title will be something meaningless such as 'Town and city and provincial directory' and the document will propose a plain type entry at a fancy price, such as £20 or $140. Some care must however be exercised in giving advice; often it is sufficient to say 'We have never heard of this directory'; but when in doubt the librarian should consult the ABDP or any of the organisations that are constantly keeping watch for advertising malpractices of all kinds—the Advertising Association, Incorporated Society of British Advertisers, and the Company Fraud Squad at Scotland Yard.

9 Major collections of directories

Directories figure largely in the stocks of commercial departments of the major public libraries in the UK; those of the City Business Library and Manchester come very close to being complete collections of all British directories currently available.

Stocks of overseas directories in public libraries vary greatly according to the nature of demand and the funds available. London benefits from having the very extensive range at the City Business Library, which includes financial yearbooks and investors' services for most countries; also the equally large collection at the Statistics and Market Intelligence Library of the Department of Trade and Industry, and others at the London Chamber of Commerce and at the World Trade Centre.

Business librarians are occasionally asked for locations of long files of directories. Outside the British Museum, which naturally possesses extensive—but not necessarily unbroken—runs of both British and overseas directories, there are important collections at Guildhall Library and at Manchester Public Library, both of them including many rare and possibly unique items. But consolidated files of many specialised trade directories published between 1850 and 1970 are far rarer than might be supposed, and in order to assist the serious researcher the business librarian should endeavour to keep a record of any accessible files in business houses and other organisations in his area.

10 Bibliographies

a) current material. Until comparatively recently the only bibliographies of extant directories were the lists included in *Willing's press guide* and the *Newspaper press directory*. Thanks largely to encouragement and criticism of librarians who use it, *Current British directories* has, since its first appearance in 1955, developed into an extremely comprehensive guide to directories and to much more material that can be used in answering directory enquiries; as the description of each directory indicates the extent of the information given about each organisation listed, the user is fully informed about the suitability of any specific directory; and the analytical subject headings in the index have been chosen and grouped in order to give the maximum assistance in searches for lists eg, of trade names, clubs or wholesalers.

Similar in purpose, but differing in content and arrangement, are *Current European directories* and *Current African directories*; CBD Research Ltd also plan a *Current Asian and Australasian directories*. From the same publisher also comes *European Companies*, which describes in more detail the financial yearbooks and investors services of Europe (including Great Britain and Ireland), and contains extensive information on numerous other sources of company data.

Outside the UK, bibliographies of directories are few and far between. France, however, has three: i) *Répertoire national des annuaires français*, which lists all directories of which editions have been received in the Bibliothèque Nationale; a meticulous bibliography, but lacking any descriptions of the contents of the several thousand 'annuaires' listed. ii) *Répertoire d'annuaires français*, published by the Chambre de Commerce et d'Industrie de Paris; designed as a working guide to the chamber's directory stock, and including brief description of the contents of each title. iii) *Annuaire des annuaires*; list of the members of the Chambre Syndicale des Editeurs d'Annuaires and of the directories they publish.

In Germany the Verband Deutscher Adressbuchverleger issues regularly an official list of members which includes descriptions and prices of their directories.

The *Guide to American directories* published by B Klein Publications Inc, New York, describes some 4,000 directories published in the USA, including the all-important 'directory issues' of periodicals; entries are broadly classified, and there is an alphabetical index of titles.

b) retrospective. There are two important historical bibliographies of directories: i) *Guide to the national and provincial directories of England & Wales, excluding London, published before 1856*, by Jane E Norton. Royal Historical Society, 1950 and ii) *The London directories 1677–1875*, a bibliography with notes on their origin and development, by Charles W F Goss. Denis Archer, 1932.

Chapter 6

Statistics and market research resources: bibliographies, guides, abstracts and indexes

Frank Cochrane

Statistical data is a clearly defined category of information and is required, daily, not only by businessmen, but also by a wide range of other enquirers. It is a relatively simple concept, numerical facts measuring some aspect of human activity, usually economic, but increasingly social; collected systematically and presented in the form of tables, graphs, pie diagrams and in many other ways. All librarians are used to questions which begin How many . . . ?, What percentage . . . ? and the inevitable comparisons—Do the French have more . . . than the Italians? The complexity lies in the enormous growth in output of statistical data and hence publications, on a world wide scale; and its concomitant increased use by all sections of the community, especially businessmen, market researchers and exporters.

Statistics are used for macro economic analysis, and in marketing to compare a company's performance against general sales trends, to estimate the likely number of customers, to show trends in consumer expenditure, for test marketing and to survey the 'competition'. Wider applications in the management field, include contract work, purchasing policy, costing, investment and the labour situation. It is therefore essential that all librarians and particularly those in commercial concerns have some knowledge of what is available. This chapter, and the following two, will discuss the bibliography of the subject—how to find a publication and/or source (unpublished but accessible data are important); the statistics of international organisations, overseas countries and the United Kingdom; touch briefly on market research sources, and will conclude with some notes on the acquisition of the material. References to 'HMSO' in details of publications of certain international organisations indicates the agency in the United Kingdom of Her Majesty's Stationery Office. Other agencies will be operative elsewhere.

Bibliographies and guides

Statistics unfortunately are not as well documented as science and technology with its elaborate bibliographical and abstracting systems. There is no universal index where one can look up any subject and be led to the appropriate line, table and publication. However there have been improvements in recent years and the number of sources containing guidance on statistical literature has increased.

International organisations and national governments list their statistical output in the following ways—a) in general catalogues of organisation or government publications, eg, Organisation for Economic Co-operation and Development (OECD) *Catalogue of publications* (biennial); b) in separate catalogues, eg, *Statistics Canada catalogue* (annually); c) as guides to locating and using data, eg, US Department of Commerce Bureau of the Census *Guide to foreign trade statistics* (annually); German Federal Republic Federal Statistical Office *Survey of German federal statistics* (1971); d) as lists in statistical publications, especially in general statistical yearbooks, eg, Netherlands Central Bureau of Statistics *Statistical yearbook of the Netherlands*; and e) reports of statistical departments, eg, South Africa Department of Statistics *Annual report of the Statistics Council and of the Secretary for Statistics*.

Some statistical libraries issue accessions lists which can be used for checking and selection. Examples are: Netherlands Central Bureau of Statistics Library *List of accessions* (monthly); Inter-American Statistical Institute *Monthly list of publications received*; United Nations (UN) Economic Commission for Africa Library *New acquisitions in the UNECA Library* (bimonthly), and US Department of Commerce Social and Economic Statistics Administration *Library notes* (monthly).

The best known works on statistical sources are Joan M Harvey's series of excellent guides *Statistics Africa* (1970), *Statistics America* (1973), *Statistics Europe* (2nd ed 1972) and *Asia and Australasia*

(1974), all published by CBD Research. This series describes not only the major sources, international and for each individual country, but also briefly describes the official statistical organisation in each country, with entries for the best bibliographical tools and details of libraries where the publications can be consulted.

Useful UN guides are the *Bibliography of industrial and distributive trade statistics* (HMSO 1967 UN Statistical papers Series M No 36 Rev 3), *National statistical publications issued in 1966* (Statistical Commission and Economic Commission for Europe 1969), and UN Economic Commission for Asia and the Far East *Guide to basic statistics in countries of the ECAFE region* (2nd ed 1969). In 1973 the US company R R Bowker introduced *International bibliography, information, documentation* (IBID)—a new 'quarterly service that helps you find and order a whole new world of materials published by international organisations within the United Nations system'. As the service covers statistical methods and statistics and includes such bodies as the Food and Agriculture Organisation (FAO), the International Labour Organization (ILO), the International Monetary Fund (IMF) and the World Health Organisation (WHO), it should be a valuable addition to existing bibliographic sources.

The Department of Trade in its series *Hints to businessmen* lists the basic statistical titles of the country concerned; and the Department of Industry's Statistics and Market Intelligence Library has issued three bibliographies—*Sources of statistics: European Free Trade Area* (1971); *The European Economic Community* (1971) and *The Motor industry (1971)*.

Other useful but somewhat dated guides are the GATT (General Agreement on Tariffs and Trade), *Compendium of sources: basic commodity statistics* (International Trade Centre 1967), *Compendium of sources: international trade statistics* (International Trade Centre 1967), *International population census bibliography* (7 volumes University of Texas 1965–68) and J Ball *Foreign statistical documents* (Stanford University 1967). More recent works are *Published data on European industrial markets* (Industrial Aids Ltd 1974), G A Burrington *How to find out about statistics* (Pergamon 1972), P Wasserman *Statistics sources* (4th ed Gale 1974) and J Fletcher *The use of economics literature* (London, Butterworths 1971; Hamden, Conn, Archon) which contains chapters on US government publications, international organisations' publications, and economic statistics. Subject coverage can be obtained from such publications as *Sources and availability of statistics: a reference manual* produced by the ORGALIME (the Organisme de Liaison des Industries Métalliques Européennes) working group 'statistics' (The British Mechanical Engineering Confederation 1973). This list is by no means exhaustive and additional titles can be traced in Miss Harvey's books.

The Commission of the European Communities
The statistical activities of the communities (ie, the European Coal and Steel Community (ECSC), the European Atomic Energy Community (EAEC or Euratom), the European Economic Community (EEC), are coordinated by the Statistical Office of the European Communities (SOEC) in Luxemburg. The office collects, analyses and issues statistics from member countries. Its output is described in Harvey's *Statistics Europe*, the DTI bibliography *The European Economic Community*, the *Catalogue of European Community publications 1952–1971* (Office for Official Publications of the European Communities 1972), the *Bulletin of the European Communities* (eleven numbers per year, Office for Official Publications of the European Communities) and titles are also regularly listed in such SOEC (or as they now describe themselves Eurostat) publications as *General statistics: monthly bulletin* (SOEC). Current checking can also be carried out from HMSO lists, and developments in community statistics are monitored in the Central Statistical Office (CSO) *Statistical news* (quarterly HMSO) which contained in the May 1973 issue a selected bibliography by I B Beesley (1).

The United Kingdom
Guides to statistical sources for the United Kingdom have existed for many years (in fact more than most people imagine), but there has never been any real coordination and some are now very much out of date.

The principal retrospective works are—the Permanent Consultative Committee on Official Statistics *Guide to current official statistics* (annually HMSO 1922–1938), this pre war survey was a systematic and comprehensive description of statistics appearing in all official publications. A new and similarly comprehensive guide is now being produced by the Central Statistical Office (CSO) and should be available during 1975; it will be an annual publication with a classified arrangement. Between 1948 and 1961 the Inter-departmental Committee on Social and Economic Research published six surveys known as *Guides to official sources* and the aim of each title was to assist users of statistics by providing detailed accounts of the kind of material which could be found in official reports and papers. Although now dated they are still useful especially for details of pre war series and comprise the following volumes; No 1—*Labour statistics* (HMSO 1949 revised 1958), No 2—*Census reports of Great Britain 1801–1931* (HMSO 1951), No 3—*Local government statistics* (HMSO 1953), No 4—*A Guide to official sources of agricultural and food statistics* (HMSO 1958) new edition 1969 (*Studies in official statistics* No 14), No 5—*Social security statistics* (HMSO 1961), No 6—*Census of production reports* (HMSO 1961). *Studies in official statistics* is a series of CSO publications first issued in 1949 and still going strong. The studies have surveyed different statistical activities such as 'input—output tables' and the 'index of industrial production', but for librarians the most important are No 13—*National accounts statistics: sources and methods* (HMSO 1968), No 14—*Agricultural and food statistics: a guide to official sources* (HMSO 1969) and No 20—*List of principal statistical series and publications* (HMSO 1972—revised and reprinted in 1974), which replaces No 11—*List of principal statistical series available* (HMSO 1965). This new CSO list is currently the best guide to official UK statistics and will probably remain so until the new comprehensive CSO work is published. The first part arranges by broad subject group, eg, labour, the principal statistical series, giving the frequency of each series and the first published source of the data. Brief notes on the nature and coverage of many series are given and a list of publications is also provided. A welcome addition is the provision of a subject index and amendments to the *List* are given regularly in *Statistical news*, which also carries notes on statistical developments and publications, mainly for the United Kingdom and increasingly on the international front.

Other official guides are available: particularly important are the two CSO pamphlets *Government statistics* (annually CSO) which gives a brief sketch of the existing UK Government Statistical Service (GSS) and a valuable list of telephone enquiry points; and *Profit from facts* (CSO 1972) an attractive guide designed to persuade businessmen and others to use profitably the statistics compiled from information they often supply and for the collection and analysis of which in any case they pay out of taxes. The case study approach used is simple to follow and helpful to all librarians working in this field. Free copies of both pamphlets can be obtained from the CSO Press and Information Service, Great George Street, London SW1P 3AQ (Telephone 01-930 5422). Current selection of UK official statistical titles can of course be carried out from HMSO lists and some official and non-official publications can be identified from the *British national bibliography*.

A great deal of unpublished statistical data are available in this country mainly from government departments, and details of the appropriate section can usually be obtained from *Government statistics, The civil service year book* (annually Civil Service Department HMSO); or by contacting the CSO or the Statistics and Market Intelligence Library. A *Guide to government data: a survey of unpublished social science material in departmental libraries* has been prepared by the British Library of Political and Economic Science and was published by Macmillan in 1974. It provides reference workers in the social sciences with an annotated list of unpublished material dating from 1940 held in the libraries of most of the major government departments.

Semi-official bodies too have in recent years been active and some of the Economic Development Committees of the National Economic Development Office have produced guides, eg, *Electronic industry statistics and their sources* (NEDO 1968), *Distributive trade statistics: a guide to official sources* (HMSO 1970) and *Food statistics: a guide to the major official and unofficial UK sources* (NEDO 1969).

There are also many non-official guides ranging from the basically bibliographical librarians' tools to economic textbooks. The major retrospective work is *The Sources and nature of the statistics of the United Kingdom* (2 volumes Oliver and Boyd 1952 and 1957) edited by M G Kendall and originally published as a series of articles in the *Journal of the Royal Statistical Society*. Its merit lies in the detailed descriptions by subject experts of statistics such as overseas trade, labour, transport and specific commodities, eg, rubber. Preparation of a more extensive revision of Kendall has been under way for some time and what will virtually be a new compilation called *Reviews of UK statistical sources* is in course of publication. This revision edited by Professor W F Maunder, jointly for the Royal Statistical Society and the Social Science Research Council is published by Heinemann Educational Books. It is hoped that each volume of the new series will contain two reviews and the following titles are published or imminent at the time of writing: *Personal social services and voluntary organisations, Health and social security, Housing in Great Britain and housing in Northern Ireland, Leisure and tourism.* Other topics on which work is currently in progress are: *Construction, Engineering, Personal incomes, Land use, Town and country planning, Wealth, Road passenger transport* and a *Survey of general sources.*

The Committee of Librarians and Statisticians (a joint Library Association/Royal Statistical Society Committee) has produced several very important and useful guides, beginning in 1968 with a list of *Recommended basic statistical sources for community use*, first issued in the *Library Association record* (2) with subsequent pamphlet editions published by the Library Association in 1969 and 1971. The Committee's research programme has also resulted in the production of two substantial items, one in 1970 *Economic statistics collection: a directory of research resources in the United Kingdom for business, industry and public affairs* (Library Association); and one in 1972 *A Union list of statistical serials in British libraries* (Library Association). The *Journal of the Royal Statistical Society Series A (General)* (quarterly, the Royal Statistical Society) is of course another very valuable source of information on current statistical developments.

The handiest librarian's guide is Joan M Harvey's *Sources of statistics* (2nd ed. London, Bingley; Hamden, Conn, Linnet Books 1971), and others designed principally for market researchers and economists but which can be read with profit by librarians are—B Marlow *Charting the British economy* (Longmans 1968), R J Nicolson *Economic statistics and economic problems* (McGraw-Hill 1969), W R Crow *Index numbers: theory and applications* (Macdonald and Evans 1965), E Devons *Introduction to British economic statistics* (CUP 1956), B Benjamin *The Population census* (Heinemann 1970), *Published data on European industrial markets* (Industrial Aids Ltd 1974), C Hull *Principal sources of marketing information* (The Thompson Organisation 1973), B Edwards *Sources of economic and business statistics* (Heinemann 1972), F M M Lewes *Statistics of the British economy* (Allen and Unwin 1967) and C A Blyth *The Use of economic statistics* (Allen and Unwin 1966).

Abstracting and indexing services
Statistical data can appear in many different forms of publication. In

addition to the ever increasing number of normal statistical sources, statistics are found as a single supporting table or set of tables in monographs, reports (both governmental and non-governmental), newspapers, atlases, and serials (especially technical, economic and trade). There are abstracting services which enable some of this material to be retrieved but the point has already been made that these are not as well organised as those available in science and technology. Neither are they widely available in libraries in the UK.

A very important development has been the recent introduction by the US company Congressional Information Service of the *American statistics index*. This is a comprehensive guide and index to the statistical publications of the US government published in annual volumes with monthly supplements and cumulative indexes at a current annual cost abroad of $490. Part one is the index arranged by subjects, names and categories, eg, geographic, and part two the abstracts of items indexed giving bibliographical details. The first edition 1973 dealt mainly with social statistics, ie, those concerned with people and the 1974 edition will be expanded to take in the more familiar economic activities such as trade and production. A microfiche library of the material indexed has been produced and the 1973/1974 edition is available at a cost of about £9,000. The Congressional Information Service is at 600 Montgomery Building Washington DC 20014 USA. The *American statistics index* microfiche library has been ordered by the British Library Lending Division and was expected to come into service late in 1974. Libraries will be able to borrow copies of the fiches, which will cover the basic as well as the current *Federal statistical sources*. Chadwyck-Healey Ltd, 45 South Street, Bishops Stortford, Hertfordshire, is the publisher for two new and important collections, *British government publications containing statistics 1801–1965 on microfilm* and *European official statistical serials on microfiche*.

Another US company, Predicasts Inc (200 University Circle Research Center 11001 Cedar Avenue, Cleveland Ohio 44 106 USA) is a prolific producer of business information and statistical abstracting services. The most useful and significant for the business librarian are the statistical abstracts *Worldcasts* and *Predicasts:* the indexes *F & S International index* (cumulative service) a world wide article index arranged by company, by country and by industry, and *F & S Index of corporations and industries* (cumulative service) a US article index arranged by company, industry and products; and the business services *Chemical market abstracts* (monthly) and *Electronics market abstracts* (monthly) which are the more familiar digests of articles on these industries from foreign and US publications. *Worldcasts* appears in two parts of four volumes each annually. The regional volumes are arranged by country and contain forecast abstracts plus outlook summary sheets for detailed products, industries and general economic factors. The product volumes are systematically arranged by product (according to the US standard industrial classification, the system used in all Predicast publications). Information includes historical and projected data on capacities, production, shipments, sales and distribution. *Predicasts* (quarterly) covers the United States and provides forecast abstracts from over 1000 different sources on detailed products, industries and the economy as a whole.

Other notable American titles are the long established *Public affairs information service bulletin* (weekly Public Affairs Information Service Inc) which indexes statistical articles from a world wide range of English language economic journals, monographs and reports; the *Public affairs information service foreign language index* (quarterly Public Affairs Information Service Inc) is of more recent origin than *PAIS bulletin* and indexes library materials in the fields of economics (including statistical references) and public affairs published in languages other than English; the *Business periodicals index* (monthly H W Wilson) of articles on specific topics from an extensive range of mainly English language economic and commercial journals, and *Chemical industry notes* (weekly American Chemical Society) extracts of articles from key trade and industrial periodicals, categories covered include production trends, pricing, marketing and sales. The Dutch publishers of *Economic abstracts* have from January 1974 commenced a new journal *Economic titles* (semi-monthly Martinus Nijhoff, The Hague). Compiled by the Library and Documentation Center of the Economic Information Service (Netherlands Ministry of Economic Affairs) it aims to select and index articles of business, market and statistical interest from more than 2500 of the world's leading economic periodicals, trade magazines, bank reviews, professional journals, books and special studies covering different sectors of industry and in addition will make the contents available on magnetic tape.

The UK has been slow to develop similar indexing services but as the demand for business information grows they are beginning to develop and the following are particularly appropriate. *Commercial food information* (monthly Scientific Indexing and Retrieval Service, Reading); *PIRA marketing abstracts* (monthly the Research Association for the Paper and Board, Printing and Packaging Industries, Leatherhead); and *Research index* (fortnightly Business Surveys Ltd, Wallington) which arranges in part one industrial and commercial news and part two companies, reference to articles appearing in over 100 periodicals and the national press including some basic sources, eg, the *Financial times, The economist*, and *Economic trends*. The older more established services in other disciplines too, must not be omitted in a really thorough search and relevant references can sometimes be found in the *British technology index* (monthly Library Association).

Chapter 7

Statistics and market research resources: publication and organisation

Frank Cochrane

In most countries the government is the major compiler, analyser and publisher of national statistics and more widely intergovernmental organisations such as the UN play a similar role in the provision of international statistical data. Publication agencies can also be designated official, ie, published by a country's national statistical office or other government departments and non-official, ie, published by trade associations, banks, research organisations and individual companies. The principal form or medium of publication is the serial and a great deal of information is published daily, weekly, monthly, quarterly and annually because it must be up-to-date and made available on a recurring basis.

Monograph volumes of statistics are of course published but these tend to be consolidated studies such as B R Mitchell's *Abstract of British historical statistics* (CUP 1962) or the Department of Employment and Productivity's *British labour statistics: historical abstract 1886–1968* (HMSO 1971). Monographs tend to be on a specific country, industry or commodity, often with the statistics supporting the text, and are useful when a composite picture is required. Statistical tables too can, as previously mentioned, be published anywhere—in books on any subject; in newspapers and trade press; in directories and development plans and in government reports.

International organisations

All of the major, and many of the minor international bodies issue statistical publications, often in serial form. The organisations which spring readily to mind are—The Commonwealth Secretariat, the European Communities, the Organisation for Economic Cooperation and Development (OECD), the United Nations (including its specialised bodies such as FAO and regional agencies, eg United Nations Economic Commission for Asia and the Far East (UNECAFE)). International sources are normally used to give comparisons for several countries or, on a world wide basis, are handy when starting a search and have the additional advantage of being largely in English. Industrial data on the production of basic commodities such as sulphuric acid is given in the UN *Monthly bulletin of statistics* (HMSO), and useful financial information on national income can be found for many countries in the IMF's *International financial statistics* (monthly HMSO). International publications are generally not as detailed as the national sources on which they are based and usually not as up-to-date. Researchers therefore, who want as much detail as possible from published volumes, rely on the individual national sources. It is much easier to compare several countries using an international base because the values are given in US dollars, weights on the metric system, standard classifications are employed and the figures are obtained by means of uniform questionnaires sent to National Statistical Offices. Comparisons based on national material are more complex because of differences in classifications, definitions, values and weights.

National organisation
The methods of collecting, storing and disseminating statistics vary from country to country. Canada for example has a central statistical office—Statistics Canada—which itself collects a very wide range of statistics, and statistics collection in individual departments is relatively limited. In France, the Ministry of Industry and Scientific Development conducts annual industrial inquiries but most short term industrial inquiries are conducted by trade associations on behalf of the government. The Federal nature of West Germany is reflected in the way that many statistics are collected by the statistical offices of individual states, and a similar pattern is found in Australia. In the United Kingdom, the Central Statistical Office is responsible for the compilation of major statistical publications like the 'Blue book' on national income and expenditure, the balance of payments, input/ output tables and so on, and for the coordination of statistical policy;

it has only a minor role in the collection of statistics. A detailed knowledge of each country's statistical pattern is not generally required by librarians and fortunately sufficient detail for routine purposes is available in Miss Harvey's guides.

Sources of statistical data

The subject grouping of statistics is mentioned on page 109 in connection with retrieval problems. This subject grouping is also a convenient method of briefly describing some of the major foreign and international statistical titles available which should be considered for inclusion in business libraries. The European Communities and the United Kingdom will be dealt with separately.

General statistical abstracts

A convenient way to start a statistical search for a country is in the appropriate general statistical abstract. Most countries have some form of general statistics available, the foreign equivalents of the UK's *Annual abstract of statistics* (HMSO). These volumes, which are often supplemented by monthly or quarterly parts, summarise in a handy form the social and industrial data of the country and give a general picture of the economy. Information is included on all important topics, ranging from climate to crime, and although subject coverage is wide it is generally not very detailed. The handbooks are also in many cases invaluable guides to more specific sources because they include bibliographies describing the countries' statistical output—the *Statistical abstract of the United States* (annually US Government Printing Office) is a good example and in fact has a cover sub title *National data book and guide to sources.*

International organisations produce similar volumes covering their member states, the UN's *Statistical yearbook* (HMSO), *Monthly bulletin of statistics* (HMSO) and OECD *Main economic indicators* (monthly HMSO) contain many figures on population, labour, trade, prices and production. Important social statistics on education and related fields are published in the Unesco *Statistical yearbook* (HMSO). General statistics in the form of yearbooks and international publications are probably the best standard tools for libraries which must have a range of basic material available. They are comparatively cheap and unlike the esoteric titles should be more easily obtainable. The present writer's views and recommendations on the selection of titles for public libraries were outlined in a paper given to the Library Association Conference at Blackpool in 1971 (1).

Economic surveys and reviews

A comprehensive idea of industrial and business conditions in a particular area or country can also be found in the many economic surveys and reviews which are available and often published by banks and economic research institutes. The figures in this type of publication can be condensed from other sources and are presented in a form that makes them easier to use; an added bonus is the articles on the state of the economy and on individual industries. This class of material is issued by international and national organisations and good examples are the UN Economic Commission for Europe's *Economic bulletin for Europe* (annually HMSO), *OECD economic outlook* (twice a year HMSO) and the *Economic quarterly review* of the Amsterdam—Rotterdam Bank NV issued in English with a supplement of tables and graphs on the Netherlands economy.

Trade statistics

Almost all countries issue statistics showing the direction of trade and many countries issue more detailed statistics of imports and exports of commodities. It is these figures that are of especial interest to researchers, economists and others as they are an important first step in any market analysis. The information they contain shows what products are going into a country from what source and what goods are being supplied to other areas by a specific country in terms of value and quantity. These factors can then be used to estimate market size (in conjunction with production statistics), foreign competition or indicate reasons for the loss of a particular market. Although foreign trade statistics are useful as a basis for market research, they are almost without exception compiled from copies of export and import documents which are prepared by exporters, importers or their brokers or agents at the time the goods enter or leave the country. They are not therefore, always arranged in a way, or in the detail, most suitable for market research; and one problem becomes quickly apparent from the regular use of trade statistics. The commodity required often comes under the heading *NES*—(not elsewhere specified) or a group heading; for example in the United States imports statistics *Cassette recordings* come under the heading

Sound recordings NES. Additional breakdowns in unpublished form are sometimes available (and for other kinds of statistics) from the originators, and the Department of Industry Statistics and Market Intelligence Library publishes an annual booklet *National statistical offices of overseas countries* (Department of Industry). They may be able to provide such unpublished data on request, but subject to payment. There are basically two classes of trade statistics; primary sources, mainly published by national governments eg, the French *Statistiques du commerce extérieur* (annually Direction Générale des Douanes et Droits Indirects) and secondary sources mostly published by international agencies eg, *Foreign trade statistics bulletins* (OECD) which process the information supplied by the national agencies and transpose it to international standards of nomenclature, measurement and value. More detailed breakdowns are usually available from the national publications. The international sources tend to subdivide commodities into broader categories. Practically all countries compile their trade statistics in some system of commodity arrangement, thus forming a basis for customs nomenclatures and providing detailed information on commodity flows in international trade. Commodity classifications are becoming an increasingly complex problem and are discussed under a separate heading.

Production statistics
Production statistics serve a number of purposes. They provide a valuable indication of what is happening to an important section of a nation's economy (sometimes by way of an index of production); and show the industrial structure of a country. They are also used in assessing the market for a particular product (in conjunction with trade statistics). As a rough approximation, production (or sales) of a commodity by national manufacturers plus imports less exports are a measure of demand in a country for the product.

Production statistics are more difficult to obtain than trade statistics which are a by-product of customs procedures. Production data has usually to be obtained in a specially designed statistical enquiry. Governments take a census of production or institute systems of regular enquiries into industrial output. Additionally there are in nearly all countries legal prohibitions which preclude the disclosure of information about the production of individual firms, and this leads to the suppression of much information even though it has been collected. Only a few countries produce really detailed production figures on an annual or shorter period basis and these tend to be the main industrial economies.

However statistics from international sources can be found for some basic commodities or products, eg *The Growth of world industry* (2 volumes annually UN HMSO *Production yearbook* (annually FAO), surveys from the Commonwealth Secretariat, eg *Industrial fibres* (annually) and the impressive series of OECD industry reports, eg *The Chemical industry* (annually). Organisations too dealing with a single major industry are numerous and amongst the more widely known publications they produce are, *Cotton-world statistics* (quarterly International Cotton Advisory Committee), *Statistical bulletin* (monthly International Tin Council), *Monthly statistical review* (The Society of Motor Manufacturers and Traders Ltd), *Metal bulletin handbook* (annually Metal Bulletin Ltd) and *International steel statistics* (annually British Steel Corporation). Individual countries with good sources include the United States with its Economic Censuses (Bureau of Census)—*1972 Census of construction industries, 1972 Census of manufacturers, 1972 Census of mineral industries* and the massive series of *Current industrial reports* (Bureau of the Census); the Netherlands with a detailed series of *Production statistics* (annually Central Bureau of Statistics) and Australia with its *Monthly bulletin of production statistics* (Australian Bureau of Statistics).

Other economic statistics
The population of an area or country is a major economic indicator and demographic statistics are relatively easy to find. Figures are usually included in the general statistical abstracts, and the UN *Demographic yearbook* (HMSO) is a major source. Censuses of population are taken at intervals by many countries. In the author's view these are a somewhat neglected source of market information. This is a pity because in addition to the figures on the number and structure of the population, they provide details indicating the standard of living, educational levels, labour resources and migratory patterns. Recent developments in micropublishing also have made population censuses more accessible. The Redgrave Information Resources Corp (53 Wilton Road, Westport, Connecticut, 06880, USA) is now producing on microfiche *Western European census reports 1960 census period*, as officially published by each of the twenty-two nations of Western Europe. Research Publications Inc (12 Lunar

Drive, PO Box 3903, New Haven Connecticut 06525, USA) is making available on microfilm the censuses listed in the University of Texas Population Research Center *International population census bibliography* (7 volumes 1965–68). This is being accomplished in three series—Series 1 1945–1967, Series 2 pre 1945, Series 3 post 1967.

A great deal of statistical information is also available on prices, wages and employment, distribution, agriculture, shipping and other transport topics, energy, mining, finance and tourism. The bibliographical guides listing the appropriate publications have been described above.

The Commission of the European Communities

British librarians will of necessity have to become increasingly familiar with the comprehensive series of statistical titles published by the Statistical Office of the European Communities. The future development of the United Kingdom Government Statistical Service in relation to the communities has been outlined by Moser and Beesley in the *Journal of the Royal Statistical Society* (2). Essential for any library even with a minimal interest is *Basic statistics of the community* (annually HMSO). It covers many aspects of life in the communities, in several other European countries and fortunately because of the constant comparative enquiries, the main industrial countries of the remainder of the world. *General statistics* (eleven issues per year HMSO) is the principal data on short term economic trends by subject and country. With the increased interest in regional development, *Regional statistics* (annually HMSO) is a new publication with figures on economic and social life, and gives mainly statistics available on each member state and not, as yet, on a harmonised basis. *Foreign trade monthly statistics* (eleven issues per year HMSO) and *Foreign trade: analytical tables (NIMEXE)* (annually HMSO) are the key sources of import and export data, and for production the invaluable *Industrial statistics* (quarterly with yearbook HMSO) gives indices of industrial production in community countries and certain other states. Part two has data in physical units on the production of basic materials and manufactured articles. Other important titles are *Social statistics, Agricultural statistics, Iron and steel statistics, Energy statistics,* and *Transport statistics* (all available from HMSO).

The United Kingdom

The collection of statistics by government in the United Kingdom has a long history. Early collections were usually associated with taxation; records of imports and exports go back to the thirteenth century and one could almost regard the *Domesday book* as the forerunner of *Social trends*. A considerable amount of UK data existed before the 1939–45 war and nineteenth century parliamentary publications are a rich source of figures. But the real growth in the provision of statistical information, not withstanding such important records as the *Census of population* (1801–) and the *Census of production* (1907–) has been since 1945. This growth has been accelerated by the demand from many different disciplines for statistical data of all types. This demand and criticisms of the inadequacies of British official statistics—long delays in the publication of results, inaccurate or insufficiently detailed figures, and difficulties in access to data—led to the setting up in 1966 of a House of Commons Estimates Committee. The committee's report (3) initiated the drive which has resulted in the extensive improvement and coordination of government services in the United Kingdom.

Each of the United Kingdom's principal government ministries has its own statistical divisions responsible for collecting, publishing and analysing data relating to the policies with which the department deals. The Department of the Environment is therefore concerned with traffic, transport, construction and housing statistics, the Home Office with criminal and penal matters, and the Board of Inland Revenue with statistics of direct taxes, corporate and personal incomes and personal wealth. The system as a whole is known collectively as the Government Statistical Service (GSS).

The heart of this decentralised system is the Central Statistical Office (CSO) which coordinates and develops all official activity. The CSO is supported in its centralising role by two other agencies— the Business Statistics Office (BSO) and the Office of Population Censuses and Surveys (OPCS). The BSO was formed in 1969 basically from the old Board of Trade Census Office, as the principal organisation collecting industrial statistics. Responsibility for social/demographic statistics rests with OPCS which was established in May 1970 when the General Register Office was amalgamated with the Government Social Survey. The publication of statistical information follows a similar pattern throughout the service. Departments are responsible for the publication of their own figures, initially by press notice, then often with additional detail in the department's own publications and eventually in the case of the principal series in CSO digests and abstracts. Future press notice publication dates for the major series are published monthly in *Trade and industry* and *Economic trends*. In the United Kingdom the premier summary digest is the *Annual abstract of statistics* (CSO HMSO) with figures mainly for annual series covering the previous ten years on all aspects of the country's economic and social life from the climate to the retail price index. This is supplemented by the *Monthly digest of statistics* (CSO HMSO) with monthly and quarterly series of figures. For the efficient use of both publications reference to the annual pamphlet *Definitions and explanatory notes*, published with the January issue is advisable. In the past practically all statistics collected could loosely be described as economic, but in recent years interest in and demand for social data has grown. In this connection one of the first innovations of the re-vamped Government Statistical Services has been the introduction of *Social trends* (annually CSO HMSO) which in addition to the usual population details includes material on leisure, social security and the environment. Useful international comparisons are made and this title sets new standards in the use of diagrammatic presentation and colour in statistical publishing.

The development of regional planning requires a wide range and detailed geographical breakdown of statistical data. A fair amount can be found in the *Abstract of regional statistics* (annually CSO HMSO) with breakdowns of the major economic indicators, population, employment, social service, energy, production and education, by standard regions, sub-regions and conurbations. Complete regional coverage requires the *Scottish abstract of statistics* (annually Scottish Office HMSO), the *Digest of Welsh statistics* (annually Welsh Office HMSO) and the *Digest of statistics* (every six months Government of Northern Ireland Department of Finance HMSO). At the local government level abstracts are available for the Greater London Council and some of the larger cities.

Two other notable summary publications, which in addition to tables include comment, evaluation, interpretation and analysis are the well known *Trade and industry* (weekly Departments of Trade and Industry HMSO which replaced the *Board of Trade journal*) and *Economic trends* (monthly CSO HMSO). *Trade & industry* gives up-to-date figures on trade, energy, industrial output for various industries and other economic activities, investment, tourism and preliminary data for important enquiries such as the censuses of production and distribution. A regular weekly index of statistics appearing in the journal is provided. *Economic trends* presents in tables and charts the key indicators, index of industrial production, unemployment, imports and exports, retail sales, new car registrations, earnings, retail prices and an often overlooked but helpful *Calendar of economic events.*

Official statistics of foreign trade are collected by HM Customs and Excise (although published by the Department of Trade) who maintain the accounts under commodity headings as set out in the *Guide to the classification for overseas trade statistics* (annually Customs and Excise HMSO). Monthly statistics are published approximately four weeks after the end of each month (normal circumstances permitting, a press release of preliminary figures is issued about the middle of the month) in the *Overseas trade statistics of the United Kingdom* (monthly Department of Trade HMSO). The figures, separated into imports and exports in varying degree of detail, cumulate throughout the year so that the annual figures appear in the December issue. More detailed statistics (ie additional information on countries of consignment and destination) are published later in the *Annual statement of the overseas trade of the United Kingdom* (Customs and Excise HMSO) consisting of five volumes, one each for summary tables, imports, exports, areas and countries and trade by ports (including airports).

The creation of the Business Statistics Office at Newport has transformed the collection and dissemination of industrial and production statistics. The office is also responsible for statistics relating to the service and distributive trades. The greatly expanded statistical output is published under the generic title *Business monitor*, based on the old Board of Trade series of this title (4). The main sub-series is entitled *Business monitor—production series*, comprising an integrated series of over 150 titles devoted to individual industries, issued either on a monthly or quarterly basis complemented by an annual *Census of production*. Essentially, the monthly or quarterly titles contain short-term statistics of sales of about 5000 commodities in total, together with details of wholesale and retail prices, employment and foreign trade information as appropriate. The medium or long-term figures are to be found in the annual report of the *Census of production*, giving structural

98

information about industries, overall production, capital expenditure, stocks, wages, salaries and employment.

The publication of an annual *Census of production* marks a significant advance on the old quinquennial series, the last of which relates to 1968. The business community now has reliable data on an annual basis on which to make its assessments and forecasts. As the system settles down it is the aim of BSO to publish annual data within eighteen months of the period to which they relate, and summary provisional data within twelve months. The figures for purchases by industry which appear in the quinquennial censuses are not collected for the annual enquiries, but will be collected and published on an occasional basis. The first purchases enquiry under the new system will be for 1974, and there will be other special enquiries from time to time. The first of the new breed of annual *Census of production*, the one for 1970, was published as a special series of the *Business monitor* with a unique set of reference numbers C1 to C154. Subsequently, the titles from the monthly or quarterly enquiries followed by the annual *Census of production* have been coded according to the industry Minimum List Heading (MLH)—slightly modified in some cases— of the *Standard industrial classification* (HMSO 1968). There are three elements in the notation adopted for the *Business monitor—production series* codings, viz, series, frequency, MLH. Thus, *Business monitor* PQ 491 is in the production series, issued quarterly and contains statistics on the rubber industry. Monthlies and annuals are denoted by M or A respectively. The collection of various data relating to an industry and their publication in one individual title in the *Business monitor—production series*, enables HMSO, as the publisher, to offer a variety of packages to suit the customer. These range from a standing order for all issues of every title in the production series, to a subscription to a particular quarterly title only, or a once-only purchase of an individual annual *Census of production* report. Linking statistics in an old series with those published in later years is often a problem and users particularly of the *Business monitors* may find it difficult to follow figures through the old *Census of production* reports and *Business monitors* to the new statistics. To help with the problem of matching the old style publications with the new, the BSO has published indexes which link old and new systems. The more difficult exercise of locating a continuous run of statistics for specific series covering the old and the new systems, was made easier when the BSO published in 1974 an index to all products in the new quarterly series of sales statistics. *Quarterly statistics of manufacturers' sales; index of commodities* (PQ 1000) gives the code reference of the *Business monitor* in the production quarterly series and also provides the code reference of the *Business monitor* in the old series and of the 1968 *Census of production* for products common to the old and new systems. (5)

The United Kingdom does not, in 1974 have such a comprehensive and integrated system of service industry statistics and the Government Statistical Service is looking into this. The *Business monitor service and distributive series (SD)* deal monthly with the turnover of different parts of the retail and catering service trades, the instalment credit business and computer services. A quarterly title *Assets and liabilities of finance houses* is also available. Facts about numbers, sizes and kinds of retail outlets by region and locality are to be found in the *Censuses of distribution* which are taken fully every ten years and on a sample basis half-way between. A full census for 1971 has been conducted and some provisional figures have been published in *Trade and industry* and publication of reports containing the full results is expected to begin in 1974. The BSO can also provide on request special tabulations for local shopping areas. It is expected that in due course the *Census of distribution* will be incorporated into the *Business monitor SD series*. In the *Business monitor miscellaneous series,* three quarterly titles give statistics for investment in insurance companies and pension funds; acquisitions and mergers of companies; and overseas travel and tourism. Four annual titles are issued for overseas transactions; nationality of vessels in sea-borne trade; cinemas; and company finance. A monthly publication covers new vehicle registrations.

The major data source for population and households is currently the *Census of population 1971* taken by the Office of Population Censuses and Surveys (OPCS) and the Registrars General for Scotland and Northern Ireland. The county reports are now all available and other volumes are appearing on economic activity, household composition, qualified manpower, work places, transport to work etc. Estimates for years between censuses and projections are also published. An important and new source is the general household survey, a continuous inter-departmental exercise, with a sample of just under 12000 households and covering a wide range of social and socio-economic statistics on population, housing, employment, education and health, which can be analysed and presented in an interrelated way. The first results were published in 1973 as a *General household survey: an introductory report* (HMSO 1973) have now been published. Other important titles revealing patterns of household consumption and expenditure are the *Family expenditure survey* (annually Department of Employment HMSO) and *Household food consumption and expenditure* (annually Ministry of Agriculture, Fisheries and Food HMSO). Long term trends on consumer expenditure are carried together with a great deal of more complicated financial information on companies, public corporations, central government, local authorities and capital formation in the *National income and expenditure* 'blue book', (annually CSO HMSO).

Requests for information on prices are frequently received in business libraries and are often difficult to answer easily. Many enquirers do not realise that a lot of statistical data on prices (and other subjects) is presented as index numbers. Thus in the United Kingdom price movements in industry can be monitored from the wholesale price indices (of inputs and outputs of broad sectors) published monthly in *Trade and industry*. Further analyses for narrower industry definitions can also be obtained on request from the Department of Industry. The retail price index, usually referred to as the 'cost of living' index, appears each month in the *Department of Employment gazette* (monthly HMSO) and in the *Monthly digest of statistics*. This index has recently been rebased on January 1974. Comparisons of 'cost of living', say of London with Rome or anywhere else, can also be rather tricky. Some broad assessments can be made from the UN table 'Retail price indexes relating to living expenditures of United Nations officials' (published twice a year in the UN *Monthly bulletin of statistics*), the *Monthly bulletin's* regular series of consumer price index numbers, and the German publication *Internationaler Vergleich der Preise für die Lebenshaltung*—International comparison of consumer prices (monthly and annually Federal Statistical Office Wiesbaden).

The *Financial times* annually compiles 'A guide to living costs around the world' from its correspondents; and the Union Bank of Switzerland has in recent years produced what appears to be an annual and much quoted *Prices and earnings around the globe*. A more detailed and expensive service is available from Business International SA of Geneva. This *Survey of living costs* covers a total of 40 cities throughout the world. Actual prices in monetary terms can be found for basic commodities in the *Financial times, Public ledger*

101

(daily UK Publications Ltd) and appropriate trade press, eg, in the United Kingdom, the *Grocer* (weekly W Reed Ltd) and *Metal bulletin* (twice weekly Metal Bulletin Ltd).

It is not feasible in a chapter of this nature to mention more than a few of the most important official and non-official United Kingdom statistical titles. Further information can be sought from the bibliographical tools listed at the beginning of chapter 6, notably Miss Harvey's guides and the *List of principal statistical series and publications*. Nevertheless the following at least must be named, as they are likely to be required at some stage in any form of commercial library work—*British labour statistics year book* (Department of Employment HMSO), *Statistics of education* (annually Department of Education and Science HMSO), *Bank of England quarterly bulletin* (Bank of England Economic Intelligence Department), *Financial statistics* (monthly CSO HMSO), *National Institute economic review* (quarterly National Institute of Economic and Social Research), *United Kingdom balance of payments* (annually CSO HMSO), *Housing and construction statistics* (quarterly Department of the Environment HMSO), *New earnings survey* (annually Department of Employment HMSO), *Inland revenue statistics* and *Survey of personal incomes* (both annually Board of Inland Revenue HMSO), *Health and personal social service statistics* (annually Department of Health and Social Security HMSO), *Agricultural statistics: England and Wales* (annually Ministry of Agriculture, Fisheries and Food HMSO), *CAA monthly statistics* (Civil Aviation Authority), and finally *United Kingdom energy statistics* (annually Department of Energy HMSO)

Chapter 8

Statistics and market research resources: use and acquisition

Frank Cochrane

Using statistical literature

Interpreting the figures, discussing the methods of compilation, the validity of the sample, the margin of error and other technical factors is the work of statisticians not librarians. However librarians should familiarise themselves with what may be described as the 'handling and using' problems such as weights, values, abbreviations, commodity and other classifications and language difficulties.

Checking introductions, prefaces and notes on use is essential. Simple precautions should be taken to see if the figures show value or quantity; what are the units, tons or short tons, £s sterling or US dollars; how do periodically produced figures cumulate—on a running monthly basis January, February, March . . . then annual cumulation in December issue? In some countries the statistics are not cumulated from January to December but for years beginning and ending in other months—Indian cumulations run from April to March (annual figures), Australian cumulations run from July to June (annual figures).

A great deal of statistical data is presented in the form of index numbers as previously mentioned on prices. This is a method of indicating relative changes in economic conditions over a period of time. The standard practice is to choose a 'base year' and give to it the value 100. Subsequent percentage changes in price, costs, production and so forth can then be shown, and the base year must always be stated. A detailed enquiry would probably require some idea of the factors taken into account in constructing the base, and this entails referring back to the introductory notes of the publication being used.

Comparisons with earlier years are often troublesome because of changes in statistical tables and this problem was touched on in relation to the *Business monitor* series. It applies particularly to time series data. Published statistics often indicate with a line ruled between figures where the break occurs. Two sets of statistics may also be produced for the year on which the change takes place, to enable approximate comparisons to be made.

Systems of weights and measures naturally vary but the principal system is the metric, because of its use in international publications, and by the Statistical Office of the European Communities (SOEC). In the metric system the units of length, weight and volume are the metre, the kilogramme and the cubic metre. All multiples and divisions are not usually in commercial use; and the everyday units are, for length—the kilometre, metre, centimetre and millimetre, for area—the hectare and square metres and centimetres, for volume— the cubic metre, hectolitre and litre. The most widely used weights are the kilogramme, gramme and milligramme and in SOEC statistics the commonest unit of weight is 100kg sometimes given in the form 1 quintal (1q) = 220.5lb av. Quantities quoted in tons can be metric tons (1 metric ton = 1 tonne = 1000 kilogrammes), UK tons or US long tons (1 ton = 2240lbs = 1016.05kgs) or the US short ton (1 short ton = 2000lbs = 907.184.86kgs). Quantities too are quoted in a variety of units depending on the commodity and common ones are numbers, pairs and gallons. Essential reference books in this connection are *The economist guide to weights and measures* (2nd ed 1962), *Elseviers lexicon of international and national units* (1964) the UN *World weights and measures: a handbook for statisticians* (HMSO 1966), and S Naft and R de Sola *International conversion tables* (2nd ed Cassell 1965).

Conversion tables too can sometimes be found in statistical publications such as the Danish *Statistical yearbook* (*Statistik arbog*) and the UN *Growth of world industry*. The sheer mass of printing involved in the dissemination of statistics inevitably means the widespread employment of abbreviations. Fortunately many recur and readers quickly become familiar with *NES*—not elsewhere specified, *GNP*—gross national product, *GDP*—gross domestic product, *FOB*—free on board, and *CIF*—cost insurance freight. Again recourse to introductions is normally the easiest way to find the appropriate explanation.

Statistical classifications

Any examination of statistical data quickly involves the researcher in the intricacies of *SITC* (Standard international trade classification) and other systems (1). Statistical classifications are similar in many ways to the schemes employed in libraries for the arrangement of books and information. They are a convenient way of grouping facts and the criteria employed in the different schemes vary according to need.

Commodity classifications are employed in the compilation and publication of trade statistics and a number of systems have been introduced by international organisations. The United Nations, and before it the League of Nations, developed common classification schemes designed to facilitate economic analysis and the international comparison of trade by commodity data. In 1951 the UN published the original *SITC* with over 1000 commodity headings, and a revised version *SITC (R)* was issued in 1961. The detailed version was published in 1963 *Commodity indexes for the standard international trade classification revised* (2 volumes HMSO UN Statistical papers Series M No 38) and the UN Statistical Commission is currently working on a revision adapting the classification to the current pattern of international trade. *SITC(R)* is used in UN publications such as the *Yearbook of international trade statistics*, in OECD *Foreign trade* and the FAO *Trade yearbook*. Some countries, eg, the USA and the UK, base their own domestic classification on *SITC (R)*.

In the UK prior to 1970 the annual *Export list* and the *Statistical classification for imported goods and for re-exported goods* ('the Import list') used for the arrangement of trade statistics were consistent with *SITC (R)*. In 1970 *HM Customs and Excise tariff* was combined with the 'Export and import lists' to produce a single integrated classification for duty and statistical purposes, *HM Customs and Excise tariff and overseas trade classification* (annually HMSO). This classification contained about 6000 headings compared with the previous 3000. The system continues at present, but the completion of the change-over to the European Communities tariff ('Common Customs Tariff') nomenclature which took place in January 1974 has resulted in a substantial increase in the number of trade descriptions in the 'UK tariff and overseas trade classification', to over 11,000. The full text of each trade description is shown in the *Guide to the classification for overseas trade statistics* (annually Customs and Excise HMSO)—in the order of *SITC (R)* and in the Customs and Excise tariff (in 'Brussels' tariff nomenclature order).

SITC (R) is compatible (and the new revision will retain this compatibility) with the *Brussels tariff nomenclature (BTN)* published in 1955 by the Customs Cooperation Council (CCC) (*Brussels nomenclature for the classification of goods in customs tariffs*, Loose-leaf volume with amendment service, Basic volume, HMSO; Amendment service CCC, 40 rue Washington, B-1050 Brussels), *BTN* is essentially a customs nomenclature and individual countries or groups of countries can apply subheadings under the broader headings to comply with their national needs. Many countries use *BTN* for the publication of their trade statistics as well as for the collection of import duties and there generally seems to be an international move towards its adoption. The Customs Cooperation Council is constructing a harmonised commodity description and coding system based on *BTN* and is attempting to relate this to other international and national schemes. The Statistical Office of the European Communities has also been active in the development of classifications, and in future all commercial librarians will increasingly use the *Harmonised nomenclature for foreign trade statistics of the EEC countries (NIMEXE)* (annually HMSO). *NIMEXE* is a trade nomenclature for imports and exports with about 7,000 headings, which are subdivisions of the EEC's 'Common customs tariff' (CCT), developed from *BTN* and consequently consistent with the *UK Tariff, BTN* and *SITC (R)*. *NIMEXE* is used in the SOEC annual *Foreign trade-analytical tables (NIMEXE)* (HMSO), and member states are gradually introducing *NIMEXE* headings, although adoption by the UK is unlikely to be finalised before 1977.

Classifications of industries or economic activities which must be differentiated from commodity systems are also used extensively in the collection and arrangement of statistical data. The UN has an *International standard industrial classification of all economic activities* (ISIC) (HMSO 1968 UN Statistical papers Series M No 4 Rev 2) which was first adopted in 1948 and constructed to allow international comparability for such items as manpower, production, and capital formation. In the United Kingdom the *Standard industrial classification* (SIC) (HMSO 1968) has been used in its various forms since 1948 in the *Censuses of production* and in the *Business monitor series*. *SIC* follows the same general principles as *ISIC* but reflects the structure of British industry. The corresponding SOEC industrial classification is the *Nomenclature général des activitiés économiques dans les communautés européennes* (NACE) (HMSO 1970). The UK now has an obligation to provide data based on *NACE* and the Government Statistical Service has decided that the existing *SIC* will be replaced by a classification closely corresponding with *NACE* from 1976.

Language problems
Statistical research, especially that concerned with export markets, inevitably requires the use of publications in foreign languages, and though this can lead to difficulties, the problem is not intractable. International bodies tend to publish in English, Scandinavian countries issue a great deal of material with the contents pages, indexes and table headings in English and the judicious use of commodity classifications can help to trace the appropriate trade figures. The *International customs journal* (International Customs Tariff Bureau) can also be used to provide a translation of the headings used in the trade statistics. A good collection of foreign language dictionaries is also essential and should contain some technical and business dictionaries.

Market research sources
Business librarians are all familiar with the rather naive, or perhaps to be more charitable, inexperienced enquirers who believe there is bound to be a packaged and processed piece of market research ready and waiting to fall into their laps. And it is true that the preparation of market reports is very much a growth industry. Export market research reports in this context are studies usually produced by desk research at home combined with field survey operations abroad (although there are variables). The study investigates the likely market for a particular commodity or industry in a particular country or group of countries; the more expensive examples commissioned by companies contain in addition to the usual facts and figures, conclusions and recommendations for action. These reports present a number of problems for librarians. Firstly it is not easy to find out what is available; ironically they can be badly marketed, perhaps because the agency has a fair idea (if the report

is not commissioned) who might buy. Titles can be picked up from the trade press and in the *Advertisers' weekly* (Admark Publishing Company Ltd) and *Campaign* (weekly Haymarket Publishing Ltd) which has also published the *Campaign guide to market research and media studies* (1972), in the Industrial Aids Ltd guide listed previously, in the *Financial times* and the US *Marketing information guide* (monthly Trade Marketing Information Guide Inc Washington DC). The abstracting services are also a useful source. Second, some surveys are very expensive (£1000, £2000 is not uncommon). Third, they are likely to be sold on a conditional basis 'For the use of the subscriber only' thus automatically debarring public libraries, even if they could find the money. Well known services falling into this category are the US Stanford Research Institute *Long range planning service*, the Battelle Memorial Institute technological and socio-economic studies of past, present and future trends; and in the UK the marketing publications of SIRA (Scientific Instrument Research Association) and the Electrical Research Association. There are also several serial titles which can be called market research reports and are available to libraries on a subscription basis at a comparatively low cost. The Economist Intelligence Unit's *Marketing in Europe* (monthly) and *Retail business* (monthly) can be found in the larger public libraries and a relative newcomer *Mintel* (monthly Maclaren Publishers Ltd) concentrates on UK consumer markets.

Acquisition of statistical publications

The acquisition of serial publications always presents the librarian with some very tricky problems. In the case of statistical serials, these problems of ensuring a prompt, reliable and regular supply are compounded by the relative unfamiliarity of much of the information, and if operating on an international basis, by the difficulties of obtaining copies from overseas (2).

In the United Kingdom all official titles should be ordered through Her Majesty's Stationery Office. HMSO also acts as a sales agent for the publications of international organisations, particularly the United Nations, its related agencies and the European Communities. Standing orders may also be placed with the UN in New York or Geneva for direct supply and similarly with other international bodies. Sale publications of the communities can be purchased from the Office for Official Publications of the European

Communities in Luxemburg. For community documents issued free of charge it is usually necessary to apply to the author institution concerned, eg, the European Investment Bank. Non-official publications in the United Kingdom may of course be purchased through booksellers or subscription agencies, and many titles can be ordered direct from the issuing body.

Obtaining titles from abroad, especially non-official material, is more difficult. The most efficient way with official titles is probably to place orders direct with the appropriate National Statistical Office especially where the statistical service is highly organised, eg, West Germany. International organisations, governments and banks, too, can be surprisingly generous, and it may be worth the trouble of asking for complimentary copies, although this in the long term sometimes proves to be an unreliable method of acquisition. Commercial channels must also be used extensively and this means finding a good agent or even any agent in the country concerned; or using the services of subscription agencies in the United Kingdom.

Information retrieval
In practice, the ability to retrieve sought information depends largely on the library staff's knowledge of statistical sources and only to a limited but increasing degree (taking into account current developments) on the use of catalogues, guides and indexes. The subject grouping of statistics into such categories as trade, production, population etc, is in itself a kind of self indexing because if trade or production statistics for a specific commodity in a specific country are required, it is relatively simple to find out if that country produces trade and production figures. Once the appropriate commodity classification numbers (see above for notes on commodity classifications) are found, the details can then usually be turned up. It is therefore essential that staff working in this field should be given every opportunity to see and handle the material and to attend the courses arranged by Aslib and the Committee of Librarians and Statisticians.

Computers are naturally playing an increasingly vital role in the publication, compilation and retrieval of statistical data. In the UK the CSO now has an operational macro economic data bank which can be used by non civil service organisations. Current basic services are the provision of data directly in the form of punched cards and paper tape, but only indirectly onto magnetic tape. Copies of particular series can also be produced and this is a convenient method of collecting extensive runs of figures in printed form, tailor made to a user's own requirements. These facilities are being improved as the demand for services from the data bank grows. At Loughborough University of Technology the STIR Project, financed by the British Library Research and Development Department (formerly OSTI), is investigating a computer-based system which would index individual tables in United Kingdom statistical publications in depth. In the first phase of the investigation, the results of which are reported in *United Kingdom statistics: sources, use and indexing requirements*, by G E Hamilton and K I Smart (Loughborough University of Technology Library 1974), the technical feasibility of either a reference retrieval system or a system designed around the task of preparing a printed index has been established. In the second phase of the STIR project various experimental indexes will be prepared, and submitted for assessment to a panel of users. The final outcome of the project is intended to be a specification for a pilot-scale system that, after trials, could be developed as an operational system. A complementary project is also under way at the University of Warwick. The library's *Statistics indexing project* is a computer generated alphabetical index to the subjects of statistical data published in regular serials by international bodies such as the UN, OECD, ILO, EEC etc. Auxiliary programs may generate holdings lists for individual libraries of all libraries cooperating.

Chapter 9

Management literature

Kenneth D C Vernon

A librarian who enters the world of management literature and business information is entering a world of change. He can be sure that immediately he tries to classify or index information, to choose subject headings, or to file documents consistently, new words and terms will appear in the literature to confuse him. He must differentiate between consumerism and consumer behaviour, between a vertical merger and a horizontal merger, or between strategic planning and long range planning. American terms will sometimes be different from British ones and he must learn that 'corporate bonds' are the same as 'industrial securities' and 'operations research' is American but 'operational research' is British. But if the librarian thinks that the terms he has to handle in his indexes are difficult, he must be thankful that he is not a management student who is sometimes invited by authors 'to conceptualise' a problem or 'optimise' a situation.

Change is also constantly occurring in management study and practice and this is reflected in the literature. Fashions wax and wane. The two techniques of 'management by objectives' and 'discounted cash flow', for example, figured very prominently in the literature a few years ago but now are no longer headline news. 'Business responsibility' is being talked and written about everywhere today, while 'profit' is a term now in the doldrums. American management ideas were eagerly seized upon in the UK five years ago, but now British and European managers must develop their own styles.

Change, jargon and new ideas are our daily companions in business libraries.

But what does management literature comprehend? First let us try to define it and then to list some of the 'subjects' which are important in the literature. Here is a broad definition which can be helpful—management literature and business information is concerned with 1) the activities of enterprises and organisations, especially those engaged in manufacture, trade and commerce; the control and organisation of these activities and the people engaged in carrying them out. 2) The techniques and methods available for use in managing and carrying out these activities. 3) The environment as it directly affects the way in which these enterprises and organisations operate. In short, the manager is responsible for the way his enterprise or business functions, for the techniques and methods he uses and he is affected by the environment within which his enterprise must operate. The literature therefore is about all these things.

If we now take the three parts of this definition and break them down further into lists of meaningful terms we can begin to form a framework within which documents can be arranged for use in a library. The *London classification of business studies* provides such a framework. It was published in 1970 and took three years to compile, during which time it was tested and developed in the Library of the London Business School. It was compiled at the time when management education was rapidly developing in the UK—business schools were being developed, libraries were being formed and librarians needed a flexible classification scheme which was in line with current thinking and which could be used to arrange and index the literature of such a broad-ranging subject area. The three main streams of the LCBS with their constituent classes are shown on p. 113.

The terms in stream 1 are the main functional parts of a business or other similar enterprise. 'Management' in this context refers to writings about the general theories, principles and practices—and is further subdivided in the classification to include managers, their activities and functions. The 'enterprise' is used to mean the organisation, but is mainly concerned with business organisations, companies, etc. The remaining terms are self-explanatory.

Stream 2 relates to the influence of the environment on the functioning of the enterprise. It covers a vast field of literature and human knowledge because business is affected by so many outside influences. In the LCBS emphasis has been given to those topics which impinge most on business and management—economics, transport and industries, and organisational behaviour, for example. Far less emphasis has been placed on the classes for politics and science. But of course changes are taking place all the time and management is influenced sometimes more and sometimes less by social factors, law, education, government policy and other aspects of the general environment. Management therefore must work within its environment and the literature is closely related to the literature of much of the social sciences.

The third stream is directly related to the decision-making process and to analytical techniques—the use of operational research, quantitative methods of analysis, computer science and work study techniques. The modern manager must be 'numerate' and he must be able to measure, analyse, compare and assess data.

1	*2*	*3*
Management responsibility in the enterprise (the functional parts of management)	*Environmental studies* (the environment within which enterprises must function)	*Analytical techniques* (methods)
Management	Economics	Operational
The enterprise	Transport	research
Marketing	Industries	Statistics
Production	Behavioural sciences	Mathematics
Research &	Communication	Automation &
development	Education	computers
Finance and	Law	O & M and work
accounting	Political science	study
Personnel	Science & technology	
Office services	Logic and scientific method	

Rosemary Stewart in her well-known book *The reality of management* (Pan Books, 1967) has defined the manager's job succinctly as 'deciding what should be done and then getting other people to do it'.

The job involves firstly setting objectives, planning, decision making and organising; and secondly, it involves motivating and communicating with people and controlling their activities within the organisation. All that is written about management therefore should ideally have the intention of helping the manager to do his job better.

The study of management is therefore interdisciplinary with its foundations broadly based in economics, the behavioural sciences, statistics and accounting—without an understanding of these 'languages' the modern manager would be ineffective; but by using the 'languages' he can apply them to problems of marketing, finance, production and personnel management. So the librarian concerned with business and management literature has a vast subject field to deal with, but probably only a small budget at his disposal for buying books and other publications. In this kind of situation therefore he must sit down and think hard about his selection and purchasing policy, he must investigate the information needs of his library users and he must seek the advice of his specialist colleagues. But above all he must identify the core of the literature—the essential books, periodicals and other publications which are central to management study and practice. Money can then be spent confidently on the core publications knowing that they will be wanted, and the remainder of the budget can be apportioned to the various subject areas within the field of management and to the special needs of the organisation concerned. We will return to this subject later.

The librarian should never leave the selection of publications to be added to the library entirely to others, however expert they may be in their subject specialisations. He must take advice and recommendations and he must go to specialists for advice, but only the librarian can have that overall knowledge of his stock which is essential to building up a library designed to serve the multifarious information needs of his users. This means that he must, from the outset, discover the kinds of information which his users require. He must ask a whole series of questions. For example, what do the marketing people want for their work? Statistical publications? Information about products, pricing, advertising, consumer behaviour, distribution, selling? Can these requirements be met by providing certain well chosen books, periodicals, newspapers, reference works? Which are the most important ones in each category? How can new publications be selected?

Similar questions must be asked for finance, personnel, R and D,

114

production and so on until the whole field has been considered. In this way the library stock can be built up in terms of information needs rather than by preconceived notions about book selection theories. Think in terms of information requirements first and then consider whether these can best be met by books or periodicals, or newspapers or information files, or company reports or industry surveys, or reference works, or government publications. The actual information is much more important than the form in which it is published.

No textbook can teach a library student how to select and acquire material for building up a library and maintaining it with a flow of new and significant publications. He must learn how to do this on the job, by using his initiative, by consulting his colleagues, by studying the subjects with which his library is concerned and above all by having a lively mind which is attuned to the needs of his users. The most that a textbook can do is to give some helpful guidelines and tips which will assist the student to look for bibliographical information in the right directions. With this aim in view we can now consider the types of management publications which are most likely to be useful, and the more important places to look for reviews and announcements of new publications.

Basic reference works

A good stock of these is essential and the first to be acquired should be guidebooks to the literature. There are many in the management subject field and inevitably they are never completely up to date. *The use of management and business literature* by K D C Vernon (Butterworths, 1975) covers the whole field and is divided into three sections. The first discusses the subject content of management, the core of the literature, management libraries, periodicals and the main bibliographical tools. The second section deals with research materials, statistical publications and company information. The third section contains six valuable subject surveys of the literature, written by well known experts in finance, organisational behaviour, manpower planning and industrial relations, marketing, computers and quantitative methods. By using this guide the student can gain a good understanding of the total range of material significant to the study of management and business.

Vernon's book can be supplemented by K G B Bakewell's *How to find out: management and productivity* (Pergamon Press, 1970), the

American guide *How to use the business library, with sources of business information* by H W Johnson (South Western Publishing Co, Cincinnati, Ohio, 1972), and *Social science research and industry* by A T M Wilson, J Mitchell and A Cherns (Harrap, 1971). The latter is mainly useful as a directory of organisations, rather than a bibliographical guide.

Armed with these guides the student can use them to identify categories and titles of other reference works. Biographical dictionaries abound in plenty and a selection of these is essential for all business libraries. The Gower Press in particular has recently launched into this field with a series of who's who type of publications in the subject areas of finance, personnel management, marketing and production. There is one invaluable single volume encyclopaedia which has recently been brought up to date *Encyclopaedia of management* by Carl Heyel (Van Nostrand, Reinhold, 1973). Dictionaries, both the language and subject type, are very necessary and there is no shortage of these. Probably the best subject dictionary is *A management glossary* by H Johannsen and A Robertson (Longmans, 1968); but it can be supplemented by the useful booklet *A new glossary of management techniques* by John Argenti and Crispin Rope (Management Publications, 1971). Language dictionaries can be selected according to need and several of these are mentioned in Vernon's book, one example being the *Delmas business dictionary* by G and G S Anderla (J Delmas et Cie in association with G Harrap, 1972) which is a new and reasonably comprehensive tome for the French language.

A few management handbooks must be provided—they can often give quick answers to enquiries as they usually contain short introductory surveys which can help a person to gain some understanding of a management technique, principle or practice. Two examples will suffice. *A handbook of management*, by Thomas Kempner (Weidenfeld and Nicolson, 1971) is intended 'to help managers survive in an increasingly complex and jargon-obsessed society'. The Kluwer-Harrap *Handbook for managers* is a loose-leaf publication which first appeared in 1972 and is being continuously updated.

Directories are signposts and no librarian can survive long without them. G P Henderson's outstanding *Current British directories* (CBD Research Ltd, Beckenham, Kent) now in its 7th edition, is a vital piece of library equipment and should never be far from the information desk. It can answer a multitude of questions. But there are others too such as the *Financial times international business yearbook* and the *Director's guide to Europe* (Gower Press, 1973). The student is well advised to spend some time investigating the contents of these and similar publications.

Of course there are many other types of reference works concerned with management which business libraries must have—data books, yearbooks, and the usual array of old and trusted friends such as the *Statesman's yearbook*, the *World of learning*, etc. But more important perhaps there are those concerned with financial, economic, regional, social and industrial information which can be identified from literature guides and bibliographies. The current catalogue of the Gower Press is useful for selection purposes and, although some of this firm's publications show obvious signs of haste in compilation, they have provided a useful series of reference volumes which, although expensive, are nevertheless important tools in management libraries.

Basic reference works of the kind we have been discussing here will be in constant demand in the business library. The literature guide books will be needed most by research workers, management teachers and students, and by librarians. The handbooks will be used more by executives and students—library users who want a short introductory explanation of a technique or method which can be used to solve a problem. The directory type of reference work on the other hand will be needed by anybody wanting facts—facts about the economy of a country, the work of an organisation, or the industries of a region, for example.

Bibliographies

The student librarian concerned with management literature must get acquainted with a few of the more important general bibliographies. They are essential tools. *Business books in print* (R R Bowker, New York) is the largest and most useful for identifying publications and answering bibliographical queries. It is a very comprehensive computer-produced list covering business, finance and the economic system and expensive though it is no business library can afford to be without it. Compare this with *A basic library of management* (BIM, 1974) which is a short well-selected list of titles chosen because they are considered to be important publications for a management library. The former displays the whole literature in its formidable mass, the latter presents an authoritative selection of books which are today relevant to the practice of management. The

117

comparison is striking.

In contrast to these two very different bibliographies there is a third which fulfils another useful function because it originates from Europe and includes French and German as well as English language publications. *A selective management bibliography*, by Georges Sandeau (Gower Press, 1975) contains details of 5000 books and articles on all aspects of management. The compiler is librarian of INSEAD, the international business school at Fontainbleau, and he has provided us with an important bibliography, which for the first time provides an authoritative and extensive European selection ignoring the false division which bibliographers usually maintain between books and articles. It is arranged basically by the London Classification of Business Studies and has comprehensive indexes.

Together these three bibliographies—American, British and French—are sufficient to serve the general needs of most management libraries. The student, and indeed the practising librarian too, can learn much about management literature by studying and using these contrasting bibliographies. They are essential tools also for selecting publications for a library and for answering all kinds of enquiries.

For more specialised bibliographies related to the functional aspects of business and management one must turn firstly to the bibliographies of bibliographies, library catalogues and guide books such as those mentioned earlier in this chapter. In this way it is easy to select a few in each of the major subject areas such as marketing, finance, personnel, production and so on. Then other sources can be used, notably the publication lists of the numerous relevant organisations such as the American Marketing Association, the Institute of Personnel Management, the Special Libraries Association, the Baker Library of the Harvard Business School, the American Management Association and the British Institute of Management, to name but a few. The BIM in particular has been very active in producing a whole series of reading lists on some 170 management subjects. There are also two publishers which have specialised in bibliographies and guide books—the Pergamon Press and the Gale Research Company. Their catalogues are useful for tracking down business bibliographies.

Finally, before leaving this subject, it should be remembered that some of the leading management and business libraries in America, the UK and in Europe make a practice of compiling bibliographies, short guides and reading lists on a variety of topics. Although mainly intended for internal purposes, copies of these can usually be obtained either free or for a small charge from libraries such as those of the London Business School, the Manchester Business School and Manchester Public Library. American management and business libraries are past masters in this practice, the Baker Library at Harvard Business School, and the University of California, Los Angeles Graduate School of Management for example, provide their readers with a whole series of short guides and lists. The London Business School has also compiled a useful short list of bibliographies *Index of bibliographies* (Sources of Information, no. 13) and the excellent Manchester Commercial Library has issued *Business bibliographies*. Chapter 11 on special services discusses at greater length library bulletins and other similar services for readers.

Acquisition of current publications: Publishers and book lists

Management and business publications of all kinds—books, periodicals, pamphlets, surveys and reports—are issued by many publishing firms and organisations. Most of the large publishers include some titles in this subject field in their general lists, but some specialise more than others. So it is necessary to get to know these and to scan their catalogues and lists regularly in order to keep up with new and important publications. The following are a few of the leading firms in this subject area.

Business Books Ltd is the largest British publisher specialising in management. The firm was established twenty years ago and nearly 200 titles are currently available many of which have become 'best sellers' in this subject area. About thirty new books are published each year and so the firm's catalogue and lists are important selection tools for librarians.

The Gower Press is the other leading British publisher in this field. This firm has expanded its activities very rapidly during the past five years and now issues a variety of useful publications such as handbooks, workbooks, economic publications, reference works, bibliographies and, more recently, business information on microfilm. It has taken over the publishing programme of University Microfilms Ltd and so now issues in microform the back files and current numbers of some 250 business periodicals and newspapers. It will also shortly be publishing microfilms of the doctoral dissertations submitted to the leading European business schools.

The Economists' Bookshop has provided a series of useful annotated booklists which help to ease our book selection problems. Claude Gill, the other main bookseller specialising in management publications, has also issued helpful lists of well chosen titles. *Books for business executives* published by Book Promotion Services Ltd is an annual annotated list, now in its 7th year, of about 200 significant new books.

Large general British publishers such as Allen & Unwin, Heinemann, Longman, Pergamon Press and Pitman for example, have all entered the same field now that an increasing number of British writers are publishing significant books. Until the end of the 1960's almost all the most important management books were written by Americans and so the great American publishing companies, such as McGraw-Hill, Prentice-Hall, Richard Irwin and John Wiley, dominated the scene. They still publish many new management books of significance and librarians must scan their catalogues because the books from these companies are often of a high quality and are usually in demand.

Enough has been said to indicate the importance of getting to know which publishers specialise in management books. Of course there are many others, in addition to the ones mentioned above, and the experienced librarian will cast his net far wider. He will know that many of the leading writers come from the business schools, particularly the large American business schools such as Harvard, Chicago, California, Columbia, the MIT and Cornell, so he will pay particular attention to the publications of the American university presses. But the student librarian will be well advised to start gaining an understanding of the publishing scene by concentrating on a few publishers only.

Organisations

There are numerous management and business organisations which issue significant publications and their names can be found by using the various directories and guide books. Some publish books, others concentrate more on pamphlets, reports and surveys. A knowledge of these organisations can only come with practice and experience, but the following short list can be used to supplement the few which have already been mentioned in the section above on bibliographies:

American Management Association
British Institute of Management
Conference Board
Economist Intelligence Unit
Financial Times
Industrial Society
Institute of Economic Affairs
Tavistock Institute

Study a few of the publications of these organisations and concentrate particularly on the publications of the BIM and the American Management Association with its European subsidiary—Management Centre Europe. They will provide a good insight into the range of topics and problems with which a manager must deal.

Reviews

Reviews of books and other publications are very important as a means of selecting possible additions to a library. There are many sources which can be used. Probably the most important for significant publications of all kinds is the *Financial times*. Every business librarian must read this excellent newspaper—it is a fund of information. Book reviews and notes on new publications are regularly included in the management pages. It also includes regular extracts from the *Anbar management service* which provides abstracts of articles from the main periodicals. Other journals such as the *Economist, Investor's chronicle*, and *Management today* include significant reviews and notes on publications.

Many other periodicals can be used for the same purpose and the problem is to select those which provide the widest range of reviews. Chapter 6 in Vernon's *Use of management and business literature* gives a useful annotated list of general management periodicals. Choose a few from this list and study the reviews which they publish. The *Anbar bibliography* is another valuable source of information for book reviews. It is published in three cumulative issues each year by Anbar Publications Ltd and gives references to the reviews included in the journals scanned by the various Anbar abstracting journals. The *Wall Street review of books*, which started publication in 1973, publishes medium length reviews of American books on business, finance and economics. It can be used effectively for book selection.

Accessions lists

The lists of new books added to the leading management and business libraries can be another useful means of scanning the field. We librarians sometimes tend to overdo the time-hallowed custom of swapping accessions lists and in consequence we sometimes pile up these lists and seldom or never use them. But lists from a few other libraries can be an aid to book selection. For example the accessions lists of the London Business School Library and the Baker Library of the Harvard Business School would be a useful pair to start with—one British and one American. Scan these regularly for a short time and then change to two others—the Manchester Business School Library and the BIM for example.

Accessions lists are also useful for getting the 'feel' of the literature. They provide some indication of the emphasis which certain libraries place on the various subject fields. The books and other publications listed have probably been carefully selected in the first place and are usually arranged in some helpful classified or subject order.

The core of the literature

It is hard to identify with any confidence the concepts which have been generally accepted as fundamental to the development of management thought, because the subject is not only so difficult to define, but also because it changes and develops so quickly. People have different concepts of it at different times. But nevertheless there is a central body of published knowledge which is basic to those who study management. So let us assume, quite arbitrarily, that a core list of basic books and other publications about management contains only those titles which are essential to a person wishing to understand the concepts, principles and generally accepted practices of the subject. It must include the 'classics' and also the best expressions of the latest developments and practices.

That sounds fine, but the librarian will ask where he can find such a list. The answer unfortunately must be that no list exists which has been generally accepted by any representative group of management teachers or other experts in the subject. However there are three lists which can be used by librarians.

The first is the annually up-dated *Core collection: an author and subject guide* (Baker Library, Harvard Business School). This is a list of 4000 titles compiled by reference librarians who examined reading lists used on courses at Harvard and then selected from these a representative collection of recent books in all subject fields studied at the school. It is thus an important bibliography and undoubtedly contains most of the currently available seminal books and textbooks, but it is naturally composed mainly of American publications. It is also too large for most British librarians operating on restricted budgets, so a more modest list is required.

The second core list then is *A basic library of management* (BIM, 1974). This modest British list represents a conscious attempt to compile a list of the 'best' books for managers, training officers and organisations wishing to form a small collection of management books. For librarians it is a valuable book selection tool, but obviously it will not suit all tastes, although it goes a long way to providing what we want for choosing books for our libraries.

The third list is shorter still. It appears in chapter 2 of Vernon's guide as a core list of 100 books. The number 100 in this respect is completely arbitrary; but if we assume that the average price of management books (many of which can be obtained as paperbacks) is £3.50 each, a modest expenditure of £350 can provide a small basic library. The titles in this list are grouped under ten subject headings and include 'classics'—books by Drucker, Urwick, Argyris, Bennis, Herzberg and McGregor, for example—important new books and textbooks. The list can be used in conjunction with the BIM list as a starting point for choosing books which will be needed in management libraries.

Periodicals, abstracting and indexing publications
The selection and acquisition of management periodicals is not a difficult task as there are two lists which can be used for this purpose. The first is *A core list of periodicals*, edited by J D Dews, which was published in the British journal *Management education and development journal* 1973 Dec 4(3) 170–177. This list contains 57 titles selected by a group of librarians from European business schools who compiled the list from their knowledge of management periodicals and the way they are used in libraries. The aim was to provide a balanced collection of titles, covering the important branches of the field, whilst keeping the total number of journals as small as possible. The subscription cost for these 57 titles was about £365 pa at 1973 prices. The second list comprises the periodicals which are scanned and abstracted in the *Anbar* abstracting publications.

Together these two authoritative lists cover the whole field and contain the titles of all the major periodicals. Further information about the general management journals can be obtained from chapter 6 of Vernon's guide, which provides notes about the contents, publishers, etc.

Most of the leading periodicals emanate from the business schools, particularly the great American business schools which have provided so much of the thinking and research on which management concepts are based. The famous *Harvard business review* has an outstanding reputation in this field and its articles are widely cited in the literature. Others such as the *California management review*, the *Columbia journal of world business*, and the *Journal of business* from Chicago also have a high reputation. The leading European periodical *European business* comes from INSEAD, the international business school at Fontainbleau.

Abstracting and indexing publications are obviously important tools in any management library and we are lucky to have one good British service which covers the field well. The series of abstracting journals published by Anbar Publications caters for many of our library needs and is now well known. The titles are as follows: *Accounting and data processing abstracts; Marketing and distribution abstracts; Personnel and training abstracts; Top management abstracts; Work study and O and M abstracts.*

It is essential for the library student to learn how to use these publications. They will answer many enquiries.

There is no comparable American abstracting publication but there is the widely used *Business periodicals index* published by the H W Wilson Company. This monthly service indexes articles from about 160 periodicals, most of which are American and some are not readily available in libraries in this country. But the subject headings are well chosen and with the quarterly and annual cumulations *BPI* is easy to use for searching. It is an essential tool for management and business libraries.

Literature searching, using abstracting and indexing publications, is a time consuming job and library users do not, on the whole, take kindly to it. For most users therefore *Anbar* and *BPI* will be quite sufficient. But there are of course numerous other similar publications which librarians in this subject field will need to use. An annotated list of these was compiled in the London Business School Library in 1973 and issued in typescript form as *Sources of information no 10*. It has been updated and included in chapter 5 of Vernon's guide.

Conclusion

Librarians in business libraries have much to learn. This chapter has concentrated on management, a subject which is at the heart of all business activities, but managers on the whole, being very busy people, are not wont to spend much time in libraries searching for information. They usually need their information quickly and they generally do not like to be presented with massive lists of references. They much prefer a few relevant books or articles, or facts which they can rapidly comprehend. Librarians who serve them should learn to work fast and if possible try to foresee their users' needs. The modern manager who has attended a course at a business school understands the principles and techniques of management and has some acquaintance with the literature. He is ready to study a problem and knows the value of a good library service and wants to keep up to date with new ideas.

An active, lively and intelligent librarian who understands the scope and nature of the literature will get an appreciative response from his users. He must know where to look for information, he must keep up with new ideas and he must know how to stock his library with relevant material. This chapter has provided, hopefully, some pointers to what he must learn.

Chapter 10

Periodicals, newspapers and other ephemera

Malcolm J Campbell

Many of the problems to be faced in the selection and maintenance of a collection of periodicals and newspapers are common to all types of library and it is proposed here to deal only with those which are of particular concern in the business context. For examination of matters of more general relevance the reader is recommended to see in particular Donald Davinson's *The periodicals collection* (Andre Deutsch, 1969) and the Aslib *Handbook of special librarianship and information work* (3rd edition, 1967).

Much of the success of any library aiming to serve the interests of business will depend upon the policy adopted towards the selection and retention of periodicals. A great deal of the information required in this context will never appear in book form, or if it does, very much later, and so it is of vital importance that the right decisions are made. The first criterion will be the particular needs of the library in question. In a special library the interests of the organisation will be the dominant factor, as well as such coverage of 'fringe' interests as circumstances will allow. Providers of a public service may find it less easy to decide which are the activities to be represented in this form, but in both cases choice will be influenced by alternative sources conveniently to hand. Care should be taken to avoid unnecessary duplication of titles within the locality, but rather to identify gaps which ought to be filled. For example, in an area where the manufacture of footwear is a significant activity, the needs of the locality for journals on this subject may well be met by the information units of the firms concerned and by the library of the local college of technology. What they may not be in a position to provide adequately is comprehensive and up-to-date material on possible markets for the product both at home and overseas. This may be where the public library could perform a useful service in complementing, rather than wastefully duplicating, existing services.

In addition to availability of funds for purchase and space for display and storage, a further consideration to be taken into account is the need for a reasonable showing of periodicals indexed and abstracted in services subscribed to. Selection for such treatment gives some indication of the importance of a journal, increasing the likely frequency of demand for it. Even in these times of speedy supply of photocopies, too much reliance should not be placed upon the stocks of distant libraries.

Indexing and abstracting services
Research index is a fortnightly listing of articles from the British newspaper and periodical press of business and economic interest, arranged in alphabetical subject and company-name sequences. Since 1973 there have been six-monthly cumulations of the subject section only. Equivalent services from the USA are very much more sophisticated. *Business periodicals index* (an H W Wilson service) lists items in one alphabetical sequence, covers the English-speaking world, and appears monthly with quarterly and annual cumulations. *Public affairs information service* is similarly arranged but covers a broader subject field, includes books as well as articles, and is published weekly with cumulations to an annual volume.

The series produced by the Predicasts Corporation of Cleveland, Ohio are of first importance for their comprehensive coverage of the world's press. Their cost reduces the number of public places where they may be seen, but students should make an effort to familiarise themselves with at least part of the range. *Funk and Scott index of corporations and industries* contains classified subject and alphabetical corporation indexes to North American material. With an additional regional section, *F and S international index* covers the rest of the world. *Predicasts* itself (for North America) and *World casts* carry the process a stage further by abstracting actual quantities from articles forecasting future trends in production, sales, consumption etc of commodities and manufactured goods. Four parts per year are published in each of two sections—by product and by region. Chemical Horizons Inc, a division of Predicasts, publish *Chemical market abstracts* and *Electronics market abstracts*, monthly with cumulations.

The UK Library Association's *British humanities index* and *British technology index* should be familiar to the business librarian, even if actually housed in some other department of the organisation—the latter for its company references in particular. Rather different in style are the *Anbar* series of abstracts in the fields of management, personnel management and accounting. British in origin, and selective, they provide a useful 'current awareness' service, though for retrieval purposes careful study of the classification and indexing systems is recommended.

Of newspaper indexes, that to *The times* (now including within its scope the *Sunday times* and the supplements) is regrettably too tardy in appearance to be of great value for current business purposes. The *Wall street journal index*, by virtue of monthly publication in paper covers, with annual bound cumulation, is likely to be very much more useful. Though naturally strongest in its coverage of American topics, important business events all over the world are indexed here, and the fixing of a date by this means can lead to retrieval from other newspapers. 'Corporate news' is a separate sequence of company items arranged alphabetically. The *Financial times* publishes no index itself, though *Research index* and *F and S international index* cover important items well and the newspaper's library will give references by telephone.

Important periodical titles
While the needs of organisations and localities differ too greatly for it to be possible to compile a list of periodicals essential to any business information unit, there are nevertheless a number with which any worker in this field should be familiar. Even a select listing is bound to be fairly lengthy but, since the most important thing about any periodical is its content, time spent in glancing through a few issues of the following will not be wasted.

GENERAL BUSINESS AND MISCELLANEOUS
Barron's weekly (USA)—*Bookseller*—*British rate and data*— *Business week* (USA)—*Commerce international*—*Computer survey*— *Director*—*Entreprise* (France)—*Forbes* (USA)—*Fortune* (USA)— *London gazette*—*Social audit*—*Trade and industry*—*Trade marks*

journal—Vision (France)—*Which?*

FINANCE/INVESTMENT

British tax review—Bulletin for international fiscal documentation—Euromoney—European taxation—Federal reserve bulletin (USA)—International currency review—Investment analyst—Investors' chronicle—Investors' review—Journal of finance (USA)—Money management and unitholder—Nationwide Building Society: occasional bulletin—Planned savings—Property and investment review.

ECONOMICS/STATISTICS

Bulletin of statistics and economic information—CBI review—Economic journal—Economic trends—Economica—Economist—Journal of economic literature (USA)—Journal of industrial economics—Manchester School of economic and social studies—National Institute economic review—OECD observer—Oxford University Institute of Statistics bulletin—Quarterly journal of economics (USA)—Quarterly review of economics & business (USA)—Regional studies—Royal Statistical Society journal—Statistical news—Treasury broadsheets.

COMMODITIES/PRODUCTS

British steel maker—Chemical age international—Chemical week (USA)—Chemische industrie international (Germany)—*European chemical news—Grocer—Industrial minerals—Metal bulletin—Mining journal—Mining magazine—Montagu monthly review—Oil world weekly* (Germany)—*Petroleum economist—Petroleum times—Rubber trends—Tin international—Wool record—World tobacco.*

AREA-ORIENTATED

Africa research bulletin—Bulletin of the European Communities—Business Asia—Business Europe—Business international—Business Latin America—Eastern Europe report—Economic situation in the Community—EFTA bulletin—European Community—European economic review (Netherlands)—*Journal of common market studies—Middle East economic digest—Official journal of the European communities—Oriental economist*

130

(Japan)—*Rydge's business journal* (Australia)—*Survey of current business* (USA).

LABOUR/REMUNERATION
British journal of industrial relations—Department of Employment gazette—Incomes data—Industrial and commercial training—Industrial relations journal—Industrial society—Occupational psychology—Personnel management—Salary survey.

LEGAL
Common market law review—European law digest—International and comparative law quarterly—Journal of planning and environment law—Journal of world trade law—Law quarterly review—Modern law review—New law journal—Solicitors journal.

MARKETING/MARKET RESEARCH
Ad week—Campaign—European trends—IMRA journal—Journal of market research—Journal of marketing (USA)—*Journal of marketing research—Market research in ... Great Britain/Benelux/France/Germany/Italy—Marketing in Europe—Mintel market intelligence—Nielsen researcher—Retail business.*

PROFESSIONAL
Accountancy—Accountant—Architect—Architects journal—Banker—Bankers' magazine—British medical journal—Engineer—Engineering—Estates gazette—Lancet—Post magazine and insurance monitor.

INDEXES/ABSTRACTS
Anbar management services abstracts—Bibliographic index (USA)—*British technology index—Business periodicals index* (USA)—*Chemical market abstracts* (USA)—*Economic abstracts* (Netherlands)—*F and S index of corporations and industries* (USA)—*F and S international index* (USA)—*International executive* (USA)—*Journal of economic literature* (USA)—*Management review and digest—Market research abstracts—Predicasts* (USA)—*Public affairs information bulletin* (USA)—*Research index—Social sciences and humanities index* (USA)—*World casts* (USA).

Excluded categories

It will be noticed that certain categories of periodicals are not represented in the foregoing list, though of some importance and not to be overlooked. Trade journals are too numerous to be treated here and in any case very much subject to local and organisational requirements. Look out though for those with special regular features, like the monthly directory insert in *Estates gazette* and the valuable supplements which appear in *The banker*. Even trade journals of a primarily technical nature often constitute a source of company news and are especially valuable when well indexed, as is *The engineer*, for example.

Statistical series are excluded since they are treated elsewhere in this *Manual*, as are management periodicals (Chapter 9). The reviews of domestic and overseas banks are of great value (though usually free of charge) and are of several types. Those of the central banks (*Bank of England quarterly bulletin, Bank of Finland monthly bulletin*) generally contain useful articles and features—as well as statistics—illuminating economic and financial conditions in the countries concerned. Larger clearing banks, such as National Westminster and Barclay's, also issue reviews with articles contributed by experts on a wide range of business and economic subjects. It is worth getting on the mailing list for surveys of conditions in overseas territories, not always periodicals as such, but regularly up-dated, of the kind issued for example by Lloyd's and the Standard Bank. Finally, there are many overseas banks which publish weekly or monthly summaries of the current situation locally; these may be of only four to eight pages, but often carry tables of economic indices as well as pithy narratives. By receiving a wide spread of banks' publications it is possible to build up at no cost (but remember handling and space considerations) the nucleus of a global economic intelligence service. Ulrich's *International periodicals directory* provides the best listing.

Journals of chambers of commerce, except for those with national or international coverage (*Commerce international, Anglo-American trade news*, etc) are produced usually for local consumption and apart from some articles of wider interest—frequently syndicated—are of limited usefulness beyond their own areas. They can however have a value in presenting an impression of commercial and industrial life in a town or region.

Of company house journals very few, such as *Esso magazine*, rank as vehicles for articles of some importance. Others are attractively-produced public relations exercises aimed as much towards shareholders as employees. The largest proportion of house journals however, are of a purely domestic nature, serving to foster the 'one big happy family' feeling between management and the shop floor. Liberally sprinkled with pictures of the firm's football team, the managing director dispensing clocks to departing time-servers, and the chairman 'sharing a joke' with the tea lady at the staff Christmas party, this *genre* holds little of interest to any but the individuals named or portrayed within. It is unlikely that much will be learned from house journals of a company's activities or future plans that is not readily discoverable elsewhere, so there is little to be gained in collecting more than those of local interest or whose contents really have something useful to offer. (Perhaps the best test to apply here, as with other give-away material, is to ask 'Would I be prepared to pay *money* for this?' If not, space and handling time should not be expended on it.) Readers will ask from time to time if the library has a collection of house journals, generally having been deputed to edit one and wishing to pick up some ideas. Seldom is a particular company's magazine requested and it should therefore be left to the largest libraries to maintain a file of specimen issues.

Arrangement
Where the periodicals collection is of a modest size (say, two or three hundred), or a limited subject range, an alphabetical or random numbered arrangement of current issues may be found perfectly satisfactory. Otherwise consideration should be given to the possibility of display in a classified order, remembering that business library users are generally concerned with particular subject fields and might reasonably expect to find kindred journals in proximity to each other. While browsing is just as likely to be indulged in in this department as elsewhere, the needs of the purposive reader should be regarded as paramount. Where the main classification employed in the library is found to be too cumbersome for this material, the solution may be, as with directories, to use a radical simplification or even something totally different.

Newspapers
Newspapers, like periodicals, will be an important feature of the

business library and for the same reasons. How many, and which titles to choose, will be a matter for decision according to the needs of the particular information unit and it is not proposed to attempt to list recommended titles here. It might be said though that a business information service of some kind *could* be provided without any books at all, given a telephone (or telex), an extensive knowledge of outside sources and the *Financial times* and/or *Wall Street Journal* exploited intelligently. Be that as it may, a thorough awareness of the regular features contained in that newspaper, together with a background consciousness of what is happening in the world of business provided by daily scanning, are essential to any who operate a service in this field. While one is tempted to insist that *The times, Daily telegraph, Guardian, Sunday times, Observer* and *Wall street journal* are basic essentials (and what kind of *city* reference library is it that, as reported in *New society* on March 28, 1974, takes only the *Financial times* and *Lloyd's list?*) it is the *FT* which is truly indispensable in the UK for the wealth of information it contains every day. Possibly a duplicate copy should be taken so that it can be cut up and individual items filed for future retrieval.

Cutting of newspapers and periodicals is undertaken to a considerable extent in special libraries, where the interests of the parent organisation are fairly closely definable. In the public library there is less frequently available a large enough reserve of staff to make this possible. Especially where it is easier to extract money for procurement of materials from the authority than to add more bodies to the establishment, indexing services may prove adequate, though this will necessitate maintaining files of the journals themselves.

A cuttings service will supply items containing given key-words, but cost may be prohibitive on any large scale. Also the cuttings still have to be mounted, filed and indexed. The McCarthy Information Service provides an answer within its range of coverage. Here for UK companies (separate services for quoted—Comment and News—and unquoted) the principle newspapers, plus *Economist* and *Investors' chronicle* are monitored and reports reproduced in their entirety for filing under the companies' names. Fresh sheets are delivered daily and the filing involved is formidable but worthwhile. The weekly product and industry service is classified and is particularly valuable as an aid to market research. Other services cover news of important European and Australian companies and selective packages can be supplied for specific companies or sectors, such

134

as banking and property. Against the costs of these services (and public libraries may be offered discount) should be set the convenience of the system in terms of saving staff time on cutting and its ease of retrievability. Unfortunately McCarthy's have been unable to conclude agreements making a US company service possible and there is nothing of this kind available in North America.

Space saving may be achieved by the purchase of microfilm files of certain newspapers, but in the purely business context remember that their useful life is unlikely to extend beyond about five years. Clearly this is a possibility which should be explored however, where the business unit is a part of a larger system with an historical interest.

Company reports

The annual reports and accounts of companies provide the basic financial data upon which other published descriptions are mostly based. Before embarking on the building up of a collection, careful thought should be given to the question of whether the library's needs in this respect might not be adequately met through a subscription to either of the Moodies or Extel services. These provide details of the five thousand or so companies quoted on stock exchanges in England and Wales. A further Extel service covers a few hundred of the major unquoted companies—Moodies supply reports to order in this category. While Moodies offer a Canadian company service and Extel one covering the USA and Canada, the loose leaf up dated volumes published by Moody's Investors Service Inc and Standard and Poor's Corporation are very much more comprehensive. There are altogether some 500,000 files at the Companies Registration Office for England and Wales alone, so it will be seen that not only do available published sources represent only the tip of the iceberg, but few business libraries in the public or private sector can hope to bridge the gap (the *Financial times* library has around 40,000 company files).

However, there is a demand for the full annual reports and accounts of major firms and while non-shareholders have no rights in this respect, a post card from a *bona fide* information unit requesting to be placed on the mailing list is quite likely to meet with a favourable response. The basis for selection might be *The times 1000*, companies listed in the *Financial times* share information pages, all those included in the *Stock Exchange official year book*, or simply those in which a high level of interest is anticipated. Only the most rudimentary records of receipt will need to be maintained for this material and it is best filed in an alphabetical sequence in pamphlet boxes, lateral or vertical files. Often more than just the current year's report is required, but for most purposes it should be sufficient to retain not more than five years.

Making sure that the collection is up-to-date can be very time consuming, even where processes are reduced to a minimum. It may then be worth while considering the possibility of subscribing to the *Financial times* Mirac service of company reports on microfiche. By this means prompt and complete coverage is ensured of either the full range of companies in the quoted sector or those listed in the *FT* itself. For the former the annual subscription is in the region of £2000, to which must be added the cost of purchase or hire of readers/reader-printers. Here as elsewhere, once the decision has been taken to maintain such a collection, the basic consideration arises as to whether money is best spent on additional staff or a subscription to a service.

Very few business libraries are likely to be in a position to collect reports of overseas companies on any scale, though a limited selection from, say, *The times 1000* again, or *Fortune's* listings, may prove useful. The reports and accounts of the various classes of US companies are also available on microfiche—from Leasco—and it is possible to receive original reports on payment of a subscription to the International Business Report Service Inc.

Trade catalogues

Even more than in the case of annual reports, companies' trade catalogues represent a bulky and difficult to maintain category of material, the collection of which is not to be taken lightly. Their usefulness, like that of patents and specifications, may be said to be greater in a technical than a business context. Though they may extend knowledge of a given firm's products, for most business libraries it would seem reasonable to suggest to enquirers that they send for them on their own account. Certain types of special libraries will need them for trades in which they are interested, but to attempt to build up an all-embracing general file and keep it up-to-date calls for reserves of staff and space few can afford. For the UK building and construction industries two organisations, Barbour Index and Building Products Index, set up 'libraries' of trade catalogues and service them monthly on a subscription basis.

Publications of professional partnerships

As a service to their clients, some firms of chartered accountants and stockbrokers produce material which, if obtainable, would be a useful adjunct to any business library. As far as chartered accountants in Britain are concerned, professional ethics forbid any form of advertising in their own country and so their publications are unlikely to be made available for use in the public sector at least. A freer situation exists in the USA. Of particular interest are guides to taxation and trading conditions around the world (Arthur Andersen, Haskins and Sells, Price Waterhouse)—information otherwise often expensively bought from commercial publishers. Partnerships based overseas may be found less inhibited in their distribution policy and so their publications are worth watching for.

Stockbrokers' reports may survey an industry sector, with detailed financial analyses of leading companies, or be devoted to the performance and prospects of an individual firm. While advertising is no longer forbidden by Stock Exchange rules in Britain, it has to be remembered that the data for these reports is both collected at some cost and is intended to guide clients in their choice of a profitable investment—which will not be assisted by widespread dissemination. It would therefore be unreasonable to expect these reports ever to be made immediately and freely available to any public library. As yet it is too soon to judge what the future picture may be, but it seems probable that any of three policies may be followed: i) direct sale at a price high enough to discourage the frivolous; ii) marketing anonymously through some agency such as Financial Times Business Enterprises, again at prices which would maintain exclusivity (this process had started some time before the 'no advertising' rule was abolished); iii) free or modest-priced availability after the lapse of sufficient time for their investment advisory element to have become obsolete.

Unpriced stockbrokers' reports do not feature in *British national bibliography* and there is a difficulty involved in actually hearing about them. They may be mentioned in appropriate columns of such newspapers as the *Financial times* and the *Daily telegraph*, in addition to which the accessions lists of the libraries serviced by the Department of Industry (*Economics and general subjects: new publications*) now carry a section devoted to them. It is understood that a guide is currently in preparation, to be issued by a commercial

137

publisher. The *Directory of City connections* (Crawford Publications) carries, in editions subsequent to the first, a list of stockbrokers classified according to their special fields of interest.

Other classes of partnerships and companies, including management consultancies, from time to time issue unpriced material of value to the business library and close attention should be paid to both advertisements and news items, in the *Financial times* particularly, for details.

Other materials

Official town guides and industrial handbooks should be considered for inclusion in the business library, unless a collection is maintained elsewhere in the organisation. Though many are designed primarily for the benefit of intending holidaymakers, all present some sort of impression, in words and pictures, of the 'feel' of a locality. This may be useful to the businessman choosing a site for a new factory or branch office and in addition the advertisements occasionally have a value as a directory of last resort. Available from specialist publishers such as Ed J Burrow or British Publishing Company, local presses or the local authorities themselves, it is unfortunately less common now than formerly for these guides to be issued free on request. New editions are recorded in *BNB* and only the very simplest means of noting receipt need be employed if the guides are shelved together in a boxed alphabetical sequence. They may be supplemented by the addition of town surveys from occasional issues of the *Financial times, The times* and other newspapers.

Similarly, the policy as to the maintenance of a collection of maps, atlases and gazetteers will be influenced by the possible availability of such material nearby. As a minimum though, it is likely that any business information unit would require ready access to a good general atlas, as well as gazetteers of the world. In addition, marketing and economic maps and atlases may be needed, also street plans of business centres. Edward Stanford of Long Acre, in London, are one source of up-to-date information on the availability of cartographic materials. A listing of *International maps and atlases in print*, edited by Kenneth Winch, has been published by the Bowker Publishing Co, and C B Muriel Lock's *Modern maps and atlases* (London, Bingley; Hamden, Conn, Linnet Books, 1969), as well as comprehensively surveying the field by area and thematically, has a useful chapter on map librarianship.

Chapter 11

Special services of
business libraries

Kenneth D C Vernon

This chapter is concerned with the special services which business libraries can offer to their users in order to help them find the information they need. The discussion does not include external services or publications which can be purchased and relates only to services which a library can, through its own efforts and from its own resources, produce for its users.

Why do many libraries, including business libraries, provide special services such as accessions lists, bulletins, book lists and literature guides? There are plenty of published lists of new books available, publishers announce their new and forthcoming publications by issuing shoals of leaflets, lists and catalogues. We have bibliographies galore available to us and ample indexing and abstracting publications too. The library catalogue, recording all books in the library, is there for everybody to use. Why then do librarians take the trouble to prepare lists and make announcements of their own—readers will surely come and ask for information or use the library catalogue? The answer obviously is that positive librarianship demands more from us than merely building up a good stock and then waiting for people to come and use it. It demands hard thinking about business libraries and their purposes; about the users and their needs; about values and costs. It also demands an appreciation of the fact that a library's contents *must be exploited for the benefit of its users*—that should be axiomatic—and once accepted it then follows that the librarian must 'market his wares'.

Special services are part of the marketing process.

They can and do take various forms designed to suit the needs of library users, but before any special service is started it is essential to study requirements in each particular case. The librarian therefore must get to know what his library users do, who they are, their special interests, why they need the literature and whether they want to keep up to date with hearing about new publications coming into the library. It is not enough to guess at what is wanted from the librarian's side of the fence or to assume, for example, that an accessions list must be provided regularly merely because it is the usual thing to do. An effective policy for the kind of services needed must be hammered out by staff discussions and consultations with representative library users. Special services should be carefully planned, tested, launched and if necessary dropped if they turn out to be ineffective and unwanted. On no account should a library get 'hooked' on a particular service and carry it on indefinitely without monitoring its usefulness. Worse still it is meaningless to provide a service which is ostensibly for the library's users, but in reality is a professional activity launched to prove the librarian's ability. This can be a form of boasting particularly if the librarian concerned goes around telling other librarians what he is doing for his readers. Unfortunately this does happen in our profession. Special services should be designed primarily for domestic use in one's own library—if they happen to be useful to other librarians also it is a valuable by-product, but that should rarely, if ever, be the main objective for a service.

So then the development of services and their subsequent continuation must always be kept under scrutiny and painful though it may be they must be subject to change if and when the needs of users alter, or a new need arises to take the place of an old one. The librarian must keep his ear to the ground and be sensitive all the time to his users' needs. Libraries exist to serve people. Business libraries exist to serve people with business information needs and business is constantly changing like a revolving kaleidoscope.

What kinds of effective special services can business libraries provide for their users? We can usefully consider a few examples.

Accessions lists
These usually take the form of lists of publications added to the library during a specified period of time and they have been briefly

discussed in the chapter on management literature. Most libraries arrange their accessions lists under chosen subject headings and provide full bibliographical details for each item. Some libraries however prefer a straight author listing. But whatever form the list takes—and frequently nowadays it can be computer-produced—the main object in providing accessions lists is to tell users of the library about new publications added to the stock. A secondary objective can be to provide management information about the growth of the library. The chief librarian can, for example, look at the accessions lists for the past year, or any other period, and quickly assess how the stock is being built up, which subjects are growing rapidly and which are more static. He can then decide, in consultation with his colleagues, whether any shift in subject emphasis is required for the next year. In this and other similar ways accessions lists can be a useful aid to policy decision making.

But, on the other hand, accessions lists are a very traditional form of library service which has become, for many libraries, a habit. It has also been common practice for libraries to exchange accessions lists with each other and so, hopefully, to forward the cause of interlibrary cooperation and, on occasions, provide mutual assistance in book selection. But this practice can become meaningless if accessions lists are exchanged but never used.

The practice of producing accessions lists should therefore be questioned from time to time. If they are really helping library users, providing useful information and performing a useful function in interlibrary cooperation, then there is no reason to abandon the practice, unless it has become too costly. But the probability is that there are good alternatives to these three reasons for having accessions lists and so the alternatives should be examined, if for no other reason than to confirm that the current accessions list service is good. Many libraries have in fact abandoned the practice of producing accessions lists in favour of some alternative—a library bulletin for example.

The library student should examine the practice by looking at a few examples of accessions lists from different kinds of business and management libraries and then try to answer four questions: 1) can the list really help the library user, who may be a businessman, a professional person or a subject specialist; 2) is the list in its present form likely to provide useful management information for considering library policy; 3) does the list really assist interlibrary cooperation;

4) how long has the accessions list been produced in its present form without change? If the answer to any of the first three questions is 'no', then what better alternatives can be suggested for achieving the desired objectives, which are certainly useful objectives for most libraries?

The following are examples of accessions lists which can usefully be examined in this way: *Accessions list* (Manchester Business School); *Accessions list* (Tavistock Joint Library); *Acquisitions* (Thomson Organisation Ltd); *Economics and general subjects: new publications* (Dept of Trade & Industry); *Library accessions bulletin* (Industrial Relations Library, MIT.); *Library accessions* (Urwick, Orr & Partners); *List of accessions* (London Business School); *List of new acquisitions* (IMEDE); *New books in business and economics* (Baker Library, Harvard Business School); *New books list* (Board of Inland Revenue).

Library bulletins

A bulletin giving information and news about a library can often provide a valuable service for the users. It can tell them about important additions to the library, give news about changes in policy and staff, or general information which affects library users and, as frequently happens, provide a domestic abstracting and reviewing service for new books, pamphlets and articles. The bulletin can in fact serve many purposes and when it is imaginatively produced can be a very valuable means of communication with the library's users besides being an advertisement for the library and what it has to offer. It can, and frequently does take the place of an accessions list.

Look at a few examples of library bulletins such as: *City business courier* (City Business Library) *Commercial library bulletin* (London Borough of Camden) *Current awareness bulletin: human sciences and management* (University of Surrey) *Library bulletin* (Manchester Business School) *Library notes* (London Business School) *What's new in the management library* (Graduate School of Management, University of California, Los Angeles).

Ask similar questions to the ones suggested for accessions lists but in particular consider the importance of communication with library users. Regular users probably appreciate being told what is happening in the library and how it is developing. Less frequent users may be stimulated to become regulars. Some users may even be provoked into expressing their own opinions, good or bad, about the library's

142

services. The bulletin can in fact be a very valuable service provided a) it is regularly examined by the library staff who compile it to ensure that it is continuing to achieve the objects for which it exists, and b) that its costs, which can be heavy in staff time, are commensurate with purposes served by the bulletin.

The bulletin can be used as a means of communication by libraries of all kinds and sizes. In a small company, special or college library, it can be a potent means of telling the staff about new publications and giving them information which could be useful to them in their work. Frequently, in such circumstances, the library bulletin is much appreciated and is often highly regarded as an essential service by executives, colleagues and other information users. It also can act as a valuable two-way information service on occasions in a small organisation because people will sometimes send information to the library so that it can be included in the bulletin and thus brought to the notice of others in the same organisation.

In large libraries and large companies, the library bulletin has a much wider circulation but can still be a valuable means of communication, although inevitably it must assume a rather more impersonal character. But whether the bulletin is intended to serve a large or small community its objects must be kept under regular review and its form developed to meet new and changing needs.

Contents lists
Users of business libraries generally want to know about new ideas and developments as soon as they are published and so the practice of photocopying the contents pages of periodicals and circulating them to library users has, in recent years, become a valuable form of service. It is a service which can be provided rapidly and comparatively cheaply.

The basic purpose is to provide people with a means of scanning periodicals quickly. Obviously the periodicals covered by the contents lists service should be those which the library users want to see regularly. So before a service of this kind is started it is necessary to consult representative library users with varying information needs and discover from them which periodicals they wish to scan. A list can then be drawn up and decisions taken on how the service should be organised and operated—its frequency must be decided upon, a list of recipients compiled and if necessary a backup service for photocopying articles requested should be offered, provided the

143

library has the necessary staff to operate the service within the constraints of the budget.

A service of this kind is essentially designed as a current-awareness tool and has little retrospective value. Some libraries, as in the case of the current contents lists of the London Business School, base the service on broad subject areas such as economics, general management, marketing and finance and group the photocopied contents lists into monthly batches accordingly. This arrangement is often convenient to users of academic libraries. Others prefer to issue the contents pages at more frequent intervals without adopting any subject break-down. *Contents pages in management* is a weekly service prepared by the Manchester Business School Library which covers about twenty journals each week as they arrive in the library. It has a quarterly and annual author index and the service is available to other libraries on a subscription basis. The author index is a very useful feature, especially for retrospective searching, because articles by any chosen author are always difficult to find when they are spread over a large number of periodicals. A similar subscription service, but without an author index is the *Contents of recent economic journals* (HMSO) which is prepared by the Departments of Trade and Industry Library.

Book lists, guides and subject bibliographies
Domestic bibliographical services provided by libraries can be a useful means of supplementing published bibliographies. They can be tailored to suit local needs and can take many forms. The reading lists which are prepared and issued in duplicated typescript form by the library of the British Institute of Management are well known and widely used. They cover a broad range of specialised and often topical subjects and include books, pamphlets, government publications and articles in periodicals: there are lists on management accounting, pricing, interviewing, budgetary control, trade unions, corporate planning, linear programming, to mention but a few of the 170 subjects included in this excellent series.

Not many business libraries have the resources in staff and expertise to match the bibliographical output of the British Institute of Management, but it is common practice in most libraries to prepare some book lists and subject bibliographies based on their own stock. Libraries do this in order to serve a particular need within their organisation. For example a subject may suddenly become topical,

144

such as inflation accounting or business responsibility, and people will want information about it. A short bibliography of recent publications on a topical subject will probably answer numerous enquiries. Similarly, in an academic library, the preparation of bibliographies or reading lists on subjects connected with the teaching or research programmes can frequently assist library users.

Some libraries prefer compiling subject guides rather than straight lists of publications and this practice can frequently be valuable for the library user, because it helps to lead him to sources of information which he can examine and assess for himself. A short guide should contain lists of important references as well as brief explanations on how to find other relevant information. The series of short guides called *Sources of information* which are produced by the London Business School Library from time to time are good examples. Libraries such as the Institute of Bankers, Cranfield School of Management, the Central Management Library of the Civil Service Department, Manchester Business School, Sheffield Polytechnic and many others, including the commercial departments of numerous public libraries, produce lists, subject bibliographies and guides to a wide range of business and management topics. The City Business Library, for example, has issued several very helpful guides to sources of business information such as *Market research sources* and *Company information* which are attractively produced and provide clear guidance on how a person can find information on these topics.

American business libraries are frequently more active in their bibliographical services than we are in this country. Management and business have been studied professionally in America for over ninety years and so the libraries have a longer tradition of service in these subject areas than those of the UK. It is common practice for most American business and commercial libraries to issue a wide range of printed and typescript book lists, guides, and bulletins—the public libraries of Cleveland and Newark are outstanding in this respect. Business schools in America do the same thing and some of the bibliographies produced by the library of Harvard Business School for example have provided great assistance to people seeking to find their way through the vast literature of business and management topics. The library of the Graduate School of Management of the University of California at Los Angeles is another which serves its readers well by producing a series of *Reference guides* which are constantly updated, and *Information guides* which are designed to help people in using aspects of the library's stock and its varied services.

Conclusion
Obviously this brief survey does not cover all the kinds of special services which business libraries offer to their users, but enough has been said to indicate that there are plenty of 'sales promotion' techniques and 'marketing methods' available for an active library to adopt to suit its own resources and purposes. A library student can learn much by examining and comparing the services which a few libraries provide, and a selection of examples has been discussed above. Alternatively the student can easily obtain for his personal use the library guides of a selected number of libraries. In each of these there is not only a description of the library but also notes on the services which it provides. Examples of the services—accessions lists, bulletins, contents lists, book lists and subject bibliographies—can then be obtained on application. The *Guide to the library of Lionel Denny House*, which is a department of the City University Library serving the university's Graduate Business Centre, is a good example of a library guide which describes the services provided. A few examples of the services which American business libraries provide should also be obtained for purposes of comparison.

Finally it should be remembered that the preparation of special services demands time and skill from experienced librarians. No special service should be embarked upon if the library does not possess the necessary staff resources to plan it and carry it on if it is to be a continuing service. The selection of material for a subject bibliography or a guide to sources of information requires considerable skill in choosing relevant and up to date publications for inclusion in it, an ability to provide annotations on the publications if necessary, and an appreciation of the needs of the library's users. Furthermore, as every marketing man knows, it is important to present the material as attractively and clearly as possible, remembering always that in a business library it is usually better to be brief—ten well chosen significant references are usually more acceptable than fifty items which a busy person cannot spare the time to look at in order to select the ones he needs.

Chapter 12

The use of external
sources of information

Malcolm J Campbell

There can be few libraries or information units of whatever size, particularly those serving business with all its ramifications, which are able to offer a full and efficient service without recourse to resources outside their own walls. It might indeed be said that the key to the successful operation of any information service is an awareness of external sources and the ability to exploit them when required. There is no lack of guidance to library facilities, as will be seen from the reading list relating to this chapter and what follows is by no means an exhaustive listing, but rather a selection of some of those of particular interest. An indication is given of their special relevance in the business context, though in many cases their subject range will be very much wider. These are libraries the student would benefit from visiting if at all possible; many are not normally open to the public, but the opportunity should be taken to join group visits, from library school, staff guild, or sections of professional associations, as occasion affords.

Most special libraries will offer some measure of cooperation to other libraries, even if written application is insisted upon, providing that what is asked for really is not available from some more public source—one does not telephone the Foreign and Commonwealth Office for the population of Chile. Similarly, members of the public should not be encouraged to call unannounced at non-public libraries without first making sure of the correct procedure for gaining access. A number of these libraries, particularly those maintained by government departments, have divisions situated separately from the headquarters establishment. It is also important therefore that enquirers are directed to the most appropriate section.

The British Library

There is no part of the new British Library which is designed to cater specifically for the information needs of business as such, but certain sections are of importance in some respect. The Lending Division, now incorporating the former National Central Library, has extended its range beyond science and technology to embrace books and serials on all subjects. It does not offer an enquiry service, but aims to supply speedily copies of requested books and photocopies of articles from extensive files of periodicals.

A serious gap in business information provision is the lack of a really comprehensive newspaper collection, freely available to all comers. At the British Museum Newspaper Library in Colindale all United Kingdom and many overseas newspapers are taken and filed, but it is by its nature designed for the use of the researcher rather than for casual 'current awareness' purposes.

The Science Reference Library, originally established as the library of the Patent Office and for a brief period known as the National Reference Library of Science and Invention, has relevance most especially by virtue of its collection of some 28,000 periodicals, including trade journals. Trade catalogues and other material from 2,500 companies are maintained, as well of course as patents from all over the world. Books on industries and industrial processes form a large part of the total stock, supported by dictionaries, abstracting services and bibliographies. Access is open to all, enquiries may be made by telephone, telex and letter and there is a photocopy service. Less common facilities are the availability of linguists and a room for the use of readers with their own typewriters and dictating machines.

Government departments' library services

The Department of Industry is responsible for the maintenance of the libraries serving what are (at present) the separate Departments of Trade, Industry, Energy, and Prices and Consumer Protection. Of these one, the Statistics and Market Intelligence Library, is unique in that it may be used by anybody without formality and is in fact established as a service to the public—most particularly exporters—rather than primarily to civil service staffs. In addition to all the main

British economic statistical series, the collections of statistics from overseas, especially of trade and production, cannot be matched elsewhere. The coverage of foreign trade directories is extensive and growing, while special features to note are the sets of economic development plans and manufacturers' catalogues. Typewriters and adding machines are provided for use here as well as a photocopy service. Individual copies of parts of the *Business monitor* series may be purchased on the spot—it is sold only on subscription at HMSO shops—and so may some publications of the US Department of Commerce.

Other libraries controlled by the Department of Industry may be used by researchers and others only by appointment. For business purposes the Headquarters Library in Victoria Street is the most sig- 'nificant, especially in the fields of economics, trade and market research. The range of overseas government publications held is considerable.

Small Firms' Information Centres are not libraries, but should be mentioned here, since the Department of Industry has responsibility for them, and also they represent a new approach to the provision of information to business and industry. Acting upon a recommendation of the report of the Bolton Committee of Inquiry on Small Firms in 1971, the government has established ten centres in the United Kingdom, whose primary function is to provide points from which enquirers may be directed to the best source for an answer to questions on any business subject. Each has a staff only of three, but with special knowledge of official procedures and civil service personnel. Users may also be put in touch with trade associations, chambers of commerce and other appropriate specialists, including public libraries. The centres themselves are unlikely to add very much to the total fund of business information available and some doubt has been expressed as to whether a strengthening of existing services might not have been of greater long term value, or indeed whether a total of thirty persons over the country as a whole can significantly help to bridge the information gap which unarguably exists. Public libraries will cooperate with Small Firms' Information Centres however, and may well themselves direct enquiries to them where their particular inter-departmental expertise would be useful.

The libraries of the Foreign and Commonwealth Office, available to the public for reference and research, contain much material on the economies and laws of overseas countries, including government publications and official gazettes. The statute law of Commonwealth territories is especially well represented and some 2,500 current serials are taken. Within the group is the library of the Ministry of Overseas Development, which in turn is responsible for the Tropical Products Institute. Here special interest lies in the vast Technical Index, containing references to literature on the development and marketing of tropical products. The library's stock is rich in periodicals, books and reports on the utilisation of raw materials in developing countries, on which subject the institute itself produces a number of useful monographs.

The Commonwealth Secretariat maintains two libraries, for which special permission has to be obtained for non-departmental use. At Carlton House Terrace is another rich collection of official and statistical data on the economies of Commonwealth and other territories. Emphasis is on trade and production, especially of agricultural products. Materials on economic development and geography are kept at Marlborough House.

Predictably, the libraries of the Board of Inland Revenue and of HM Customs and Excise specialise in topics relating to taxation and fiscal control. The first is concerned with direct taxation systems, as well as economics and law, of all foreign countries. Enquiries may be made by letter, but the public is not admitted. Bona fide researchers may gain access to HM Customs and Excise library, where the subject range includes trade statistics, public finance, economics and administration, as well as a large body of materials on commodities and trades which are likely to be subject to indirect taxation or other fiscal controls.

The Treasury and Cabinet Office libraries are concerned largely with finance, economics and management topics. That of the Treasury Solicitor's Department is a considerable collection of around 20,000 legal works. Professional institutions and research workers may refer by appointment.

Similar arrangements govern access to the library of the Department of Employment, where the specialities are all aspects of employment and manpower, safety, health and welfare, trade unions and industrial relations, conditions of work, wages, industrial training, management and monopolies.

Department of Health and Social Security libraries admit researchers and students, and will cooperate with other libraries.

Social welfare and benefits, National Insurance etc, the National Health Service and hygiene are some of their fields of interest. At the Home Office coverage is of the social sciences, in particular criminal law, child care, immigration and race relations. Public access is strictly limited.

The Department of the Environment has a very broad remit, being an amalgam of former ministries responsible for housing and local government, public building and works, and transport. The various libraries are of interest to business therefore, for what they contain on these subjects, including town and country planning, land use and pollution in its various forms. Especially noteworthy is what is doubtless the most complete collection of local development plans in the country. Research workers and local authority staffs are admitted by appointment.

Libraries of professional institutions

Professional bodies maintain libraries primarily as a service to their own members and staffs, but some will participate in cooperative loan schemes and their librarians will usually be found to be helpful to other information workers when more usual sources fail. Researchers, students and others may also be permitted to use these libraries by arrangement, but this is a courtesy not to be abused; enquirers should never be encouraged to call on such institutions without first establishing that they will be welcome. It is a fact though that an enquirer at a public library may be a member of a professional or trade organisation, but unaware of the specialist information facilities available to him by right. More commonly he may be an employee of an enterprise whose membership entitles him to use such services. It is therefore important that all whose job it is to advise on information sources should be cognisant of those which strictly control access, as well as the more 'public' services.

What is probably the most comprehensive library of management materials in Europe, that of the British Institute of Management, is however freely available to the public for reference without formality. As well as more than 55,000 books and 300 periodicals on theory and techniques, personnel management, production, finance, research and development, marketing, purchasing, staff education and training, the library has significant collections of house journals and trade unions' publications. For members and collective subscribers extended services are available, including access to a wide range of reading lists, information broadsheets and checklists; other BIM publications are available at reduced prices. Any library seriously concerned with business information would do well to explore the possibility of becoming a collective subscriber. The quarterly *Management digest and review*, as well as being the principle communication vehicle between the organisation and its membership, incorporates *Management abstracts*, formerly a separate publication. A section devoted to BIM activities is also a feature of the monthly *Management today*, circulated free to all members and collective subscribers, though independently published by Haymarket Press. The Centre for Interfirm Comparison studies comparative profitability among companies within their sectors of activity, but its findings are not made public. Other BIM services assist in training matters and (together with the Confederation of British Industry) the choice of management consultants for particular purposes, in the UK and overseas.

The Chartered Insurance Institute possesses an important library relating to all aspects of insurance, past and present, in addition to peripheral subjects such as economics, law, finance, transport and shipping. Similarly, that of the Institute of Chartered Accountants in England and Wales includes law, management and training within its range. Both contain extensive files of relevant periodicals.

At the Institute of Chartered Secretaries there is a comprehensive collection of company histories. Other main subject fields are secretarial practice, company and commercial law, economics, accounting and management. Economics, law and management are also featured in the library of the Institute of Bankers, in addition to banking and finance and the social sciences. A full lending service for students is operated here as well as the usual facilities for members.

Trade, industrial and commercial bodies
Trade associations may in some cases be important sources of information on their particular subjects. A model in this regard is the Cement and Concrete Association, with a library and information bureau not only offering cooperation with other libraries, but also permitting fairly free access by the public to its stock of around 3,500 volumes and over 375 periodicals. This though is not typical and more modest and restricted services are commoner, there being frequently no library at all, in which case a member of the secretariat may be helpful. Other small trade associations use some agency such

as a firm of chartered accountants to manage their affairs and little or no data may be available to non-member enquirers. Again, published information can vary from very detailed statistical series, through annual reports with informative appendices, to nothing at all. It has to be remembered that, while a group of manufacturers or traders may draw together in an organisation for some purposes of mutual interest, they are likely to be in competition with each other and unwilling to disclose certain information amongst themselves, far less to the outside world. *Directory of British associations* (CBD Research) and the *Aslib directory* will provide the best guidance to what may be expected of these bodies.

The central organisation of UK trade associations and employers' organisations (though by no means all belong and indeed individual enterprises comprise a large part of its membership) is the Confederation of British Industry, formed in 1965 through an amalgamation of the Federation of British Industries, the British Employers' Confederation and the National Association of British Manufacturers. The library itself is primarily a service for CBI staff, but the information department will handle enquiries relating to CBI policies and activities, as well as advising which of the specialist directorates may be able to help with other matters. Non-members should not expect detailed guidance on taxation, wages and conditions, company law etc, but here again the enquirer may be surprised to find his company's name marked in the *UK Kompass* as being in membership. Among publications, the *CBI review* and *Industrial trends survey*, both quarterly, are available for public purchase. The latter is a much-quoted indicator of industrialists' confidence or otherwise in the light of the prevailing economic situation.

Local chambers of commerce will be in a position to help their members to a greater or lesser extent with matters affecting the conduct of their business. The London Chamber of Commerce and Industry however, includes amongst its large membership many local chambers and companies from far outside the London area. Thus it is able to support an extensive information department offering assistance in such fields as customs and tariffs, business rating and taxation, agencies, contracts and overseas manufacturers and suppliers. As part of this service the library has a strong directories section and a large collection of periodicals, as well as books on relevant topics. Aid to non-members is necessarily limited, and it is unfortunately no longer possible for casual callers to refer to journals.

Research and development associations exist for a number of industries and products and are likely to be useful more from the technological viewpoint than that of business as such. Some, like PIRA (for the paper and board, printing and packaging industries) and the Copper Development Association, have significant libraries however, and may be noted particularly for their large periodicals holdings.

Another potential source for product information, in this case building materials and equipment, is the library of the Building Centre. Primarily designed to serve the building industry, the bookstock is not large, but there are many pamphlets and some 200 relevant periodicals are taken.

Overseas representatives in the UK

United Kingdom offices of representatives of overseas territories may be found helpful with regard to certain categories of information. It is impossible to generalise here though; some have libraries as such, at others the commercial attaché may be the appropriate point of contact, but frequent difficulty may be encountered in finding anybody in a position to cope intelligently with enquiries. Experience is the best teacher here, but for some embassies a wise precaution is to avoid telephoning at what might be considered to be siesta time.

In a category of its own is the London Office of the European Communities, in that its function is not diplomatic representation, but rather as a source of general and specialised information on the work of the communities. The library is freely available for reference and contains virtually all EC documents, proposals, reports and statistical series, as well as many reference books. It is a most valuable resource for identifying the relevant community documentation for a particular purpose and, where items not obtainable through more conventional channels are needed quickly, may be able to supply direct. The staff is not large though, and should obviously not be burdened with any and every conceivable query relating to the communities where there are other appropriate sources of information.

The larger Commonwealth and former Commonwealth territories are well equipped with library services, professionally staffed and willing to assist. For example, the Australian Reference Library includes in its stock most federal government publications, including a wide range of statistics, together with materials on Australian law and the social sciences. Some 1,500 periodicals and newspapers are taken currently. The coverage of the libraries at New Zealand House, Canada House and South Africa House is similar. At the Indian High Commission all aspects of Indian affairs are represented, particularly finance, trade and production, and the collection of union and state government publications is notably extensive.

There is at the American Embassy, in addition to the general library, a more specialised library attached to the commercial section. This is established principally to serve the interests of those concerned with purchasing from the USA (a considerable file is maintained of details of UK agents for American products) and while academic and other institutional enquirers will be assisted, the generality of the public are discouraged.

Cultural institutes are not usually major sources for business information, but the German Institute (certainly that in London, though there are others in Manchester and Glasgow) includes within its range works on geography, economics and sociology, as well as some directories. The French Institute and the Institute of Spain also contain some pertinent materials. All are freely available to the public.

Chambers of commerce of overseas countries in Great Britain are a further possible source of information on trade matters. Any periodicals they publish should be borne in mind for acquisition, as indeed should lists of members, which serve as useful, though generally modest, directories. In this respect the *Anglo-American trade directory* stands in a class of its own and a business library of any size will need it for constant reference, particularly in tracing transatlantic company links.

Libraries of academic institutions

The importance of libraries of universities, colleges and polytechnics as sources for business information will vary according both to the faculties of the institution and the level of alternative provision in the locality. It may happen that a college with a strong business studies department maintains a collection of company reports or subscribes to card services of the Moodies or Extel type and is thus able to supplement the more modest materials in the local public library. The same might be true too of the provision of more specialised periodicals. While the needs of staff and students will naturally have first claim in such library services, it is quite common for them to be reasonably accessible to *bona fide* outsiders by arrangement or through a regional cooperative scheme. So the business librarian should make it a part of his job to familiarise himself with what may be available in this way and to foster contacts with the relevant personnel.

Some academic libraries of course are of far more than local significance. One such is the British Library of Political and Economic Science, which is very much more than merely the library of the London School of Economics, to which it is attached. The subject range of its over two million items is also far wider than its name suggests, embracing commerce, statistics, accounting, management, industrial relations, law and geography, as well as fields which might more obviously come to mind. A useful accessions list is published. It is essentially a library of research and not for the casual enquirer, but with a good record of cooperation, through loans and photocopy provision, with other libraries. Similar restrictions on public access apply at the library of the Oxford University Institute of Economics and Statistics. Here, in addition to wider considerations of the theory and application of statistics and economics, particular attention is focussed on the economies of developing countries, management and the use of computers. The institute's *Bulletin* is an important journal in its field.

The library of the London Graduate Business School is, of its type, perhaps second in importance in the UK only to that of the British Institute of Management. Like that of the BIM, this library too is freely available to the public for reference purposes. In addition to the more obvious 'management' topics, coverage of product and industry data and company information is excellent and there are holdings of materials such as stockbrokers' reports which are not otherwise easily to be seen. Here again the library's accessions list is worth subscribing to and other useful publications include a series of 'Sources of information', short reading lists and bibliographies, and photocopies of contents pages of leading journals within six subject areas. It is of course also the best place to see the *London classification of business studies* in operation, since this is the collection it was originally designed to serve.

The 'open door' situation at the London Business School is a result of tax-saving status as a charitable body. Another way of increasing the funds available for financing an academic library is by levying a charge on outside organisations wishing to avail themselves of the facility. This is the course adopted at the University of Warwick, where payment of an annual subscription secures access to an economic statistics collection unrivalled outside the Statistics and Market Intelligence Library in London. All official and many unofficial statistical series of the United Kingdom are held here, with extensive back files. For some overseas territories virtually complete sets of current series are to be found, thanks to the good will of depositing governments, while for others the aim is to secure at least the annual general statistical handbook and monthly digest, censuses of production and distribution, national accounts and annual production figures. Thus in the Midlands there is firmly established a facility of a comprehensiveness not hitherto to be found outside London. Further charges are made for extended assistance by the staff, and private study rooms, photocopiers and calculators are available.

A wider field of enquiry is open to subscribers to the information centre operated by the International Business Unit at the University of Manchester Institute for Science and Technology (UMIST). Factual enquiries may be made by post, telephone or in person, for a subscription of £250 per year and includes access to a data store of files on over 2,500 international companies, industry sectors and countries, and a card index of references to business contacts in many parts of the world. There is also a bibliography of over 3,000 references to books, periodicals and articles, and a calendar of forthcoming European conferences, seminars etc for businessmen and academics. Where broader, general issues are involved, it might be suggested to the enquirer that a sponsored research project would be appropriate. It remains to be seen whether Warwick's and Manchester's examples will be followed.

Other restricted access services
As a glance through the *Aslib directory* or the *Libraries, museums and art galleries yearbook* will show, there is a wide and varied spectrum of 'special libraries' in Britain, many falling outside the categories so far mentioned. Their response to enquiries from outsiders is varied too, but there is a fraternity among librarians which cuts across boundaries of apparent exclusivity. An approach in the right spirit, where it is evident that an organisation's special expertise is best fitted to tackle a particular problem, more orthodox channels having failed, is rarely likely to be rudely rebuffed, though loans may have to be refused.

Elsewhere in this *Manual* the need of companies of all sizes to maintain information units, however modest, is indicated, and indeed the range extends from the one man (or woman) outfit run by an individual with a very firm grip on the needs of a fairly confined community, to the great multi-nationals like IBM and ICI with numerous libraries serving offices and plants spread about the country. Though many of these are largely occupied by technological matters it is increasingly recognised that non-technical, particularly marketing, operations need to be served with efficient intelligence. Enterprises such as Unilever and the major banks maintain fairly sophisticated economic information units.

The Bank of England itself has (in addition to a staff lending library) a reference collection of some 50,000 books and 4,000 periodicals covering the fields of banking, finance and economics. Very short loans may be made by special request. A smaller collection on economics and statistics is maintained by the National Institute for Economic and Social Research, to which only approved research workers are admitted, though the library participates in co-operative schemes. The *National Institute economic review* is a most influential quarterly journal, its annual summary of the UK economic situation and prospects for the future being especially important. Statistical theory and applications are the concern of the Royal Statistical Society, which will lend material through the British Library (Lending Division), admits non-members by arrangement, but will deal only with bibliographical enquiries from outside.

The library of the Royal Institute of International Affairs (Chatham House) has some 130,000 books and 650 periodicals on politics and economics, as well as maintaining a large cuttings file on current affairs. Public admission is very selective but again cooperation with other libraries is good. All aspects of life in Commonwealth territories, including geography and commerce, fall within the scope of the very extensive library of the Royal Commonwealth Society, which holds an especially impressive collection of government publications. The public are permitted to use this service for reference. Similarly freely accessible is the library of the Hispanic and Luso-Brazilian Councils, better known as Canning House. Commerce and statistics are included among facets of life in Spain, Portugal and Latin America treated here.

The Industrial Society is an organisation which aims to bring together managers and workpeople for the furtherance of matters of mutual concern. Emphasis is firmly on practical, rather than theoretical means of achieving this. Its library is strong in materials on personnel management, industrial relations, training, safety, health and welfare.

Unique of its kind, the *Financial times* library has files on some 45,000 UK companies containing, as well as annual reports and accounts, constantly up-dated press cuttings. There are other cuttings files arranged geographically and by products and industries, a card index and dossiers on prominent personalities, extensive statistical materials, government publications and reference books of business relevance. Periodicals and newspapers taken number some 700. This collection is supplemented by a link with the French SVP (*S'il vous plaît*) service, which is itself vastly more comprehensive, and another with the Atomic Energy Research Establishment, which opens up the additional fields of science and technology.

For access to the complete FT-SVP system by means of an exclusive telephone number, subscribers currently pay a minimum of £120 per year, though others may still use the normal number to obtain from the library references from the newspaper's index. Very much more has to be paid for the privilege of using the library at Bracken House in person, including the use of private study carrels and unlimited photocopying facilities.

All whose work is with business information should be thoroughly familiar with the kind of data to be found in the *Financial times* itself and time spent in at least scanning its pages daily is never wasted. A useful *Guide to FT statistics* is available and repays study. The paper's Business Enterprises Division is a prolific publisher and marketer of books, surveys and newsletters, including the Guildstream package of company financial information and industry studies. Unfortunately materials of this kind are inevitably expensive and mostly beyond the resources of the public library, which is less able than a company library to select certain sectors of industry on which to concentrate interest.

Another *FT* venture is the Mirac service of company annual reports and accounts on microfiche. Here there is a choice between subscribing for those of all quoted companies at around £2,000 and, for a lower subscription, those which pay for their share price movements to be recorded daily in the newspaper itself. Such a service might appear to be a godsend for larger public libraries out of convenient range of the Companies Registration Office (at least until

Companies House has its own microfiche service in full operation). But the present system of funding public libraries and current local authority attitudes to the provision of information for business generally, preclude the likelihood of their taking up even a system so tailormade to meet popular demand.

Local authority business services
Local authorities have very many calls upon their available financial resources, some statutory and some permissive. While it may be a matter for pride that in the UK the provision of library services covering the entire country has long been taken for granted, only recently has there been any attempt to impose minimum standards to be aimed at. The government department responsible for encouraging the achievement and maintenance of these standards having as its titular fields of concern 'education and science' it is not surprising that the provision of an information service falling into neither category should have received so little emphasis. So we have a situation where subscription services can thrive even in central London, where library provision is rich though fragmented, and at Coventry (Warwick University), centre of a lively cooperative scheme (CADIG) and accessible to one of the greatest of provincial libraries, Birmingham, where concern for commercial information is demonstrated in the new central library.

For an insight into what may be achieved in the public sector, given a degree of enthusiasm and financial backing, the student should make an effort to see the business services at Manchester, Sheffield, Nottingham, Glasgow and of course Birmingham. In London, Westminster and Camden (Holborn) have been and remain exemplary, and the City Business Library, provided by a local authority whose financial resources almost entirely stem from the business community, is able to go further in some respects than is common. Elsewhere good work is done without the resources of a great conurbation, largely through the efforts of interested staff aware of outside sources to supplement their own stocks. Overall though, the picture is of, on the one hand, rich and important commercial and industrial centres doing less than they should and on the other, large grey areas run by smaller authorities prevented by financial insufficiency from doing what they might. It remains to be seen what changes the 1974 local government reorganisation may bring through less fragmentation of responsibility.

Commercial information provision overseas

Outside the UK it is largely in the USA and the 'old Commonwealth' countries that local authorities are to be found making a serious effort to satisfy information needs of the business community. For example in Auckland, New Zealand a new service of this kind has recently been established, and that of Toronto Public Library is of some significance. But nowhere in the municipal sector are the size and vitality of Cleveland's Business Information Department to be matched. Since 1929 a collection of some 155,000 books, 3,600 periodicals, 400 loose-leaf services, files on 12,000 economic topics and over 6,000 companies, as well as much else, has been built up and energetically exploited. Other US cities, such as Detroit and New York, make special provision for business users, but the Cleveland phenomenon is unique in the world.

Also in the USA is the world's largest management collection, the Baker Library of Harvard University Graduate School of Business Administration. Here some 402,530 books and 2,500 periodicals and serials on business and economics are held.

Elsewhere, in France and Japan for example, chambers of commerce are pre-eminent in the business information field. This is most marked where, unlike the UK, membership of the local chamber is mandatory to business houses, making available large financial resources from subscriptions, and consequently reducing the local authorities' liability. City tradespeople were responsible for the establishment in Germany of what is now the largest storehouse of commercial information materials in the world. Users of the Hamburgisches Welt Wirtschafts-Archiv (HWWA), pay a fee for research undertaken in a collection of around 530,000 volumes. In the Netherlands the government, through the Ministry of Economic Affairs, provides the other great European national commercial library readily accessible to members of the public. Directories and company annual reports in unique abundance make the Bibliotheek-en Documentaatiecentrum van de Economische Voorlichtingsdienst at the Hague of far more than local importance. Statistical materials are well represented too, in a collection of some 85,000 volumes in the fields of economics, commerce and insurance.

Experience of the large numbers of professional visitors from many countries to business libraries in Britain at least suggests an increasing universal awareness of information needs beyond the long recognised fields of science and technology. It will be surprising if there is not a consequent stimulation of demand for information workers educated and trained to create and maintain such services.

References and further reading

Editor's note: Contributors' citations are numbered as in the text. Other suggestions for further reading are unnumbered. Some aspects of business librarianship are poorly documented and gaps are therefore unavoidable. Again, due to the pace of change in this field, some worthwhile works have been omitted due to their age, but students would profit from examination of some sections of the Aslib *Handbook of special librarianship and information work* (third edition, 1967).

Chapter one

1 M B Line 'National library planning in the United Kingdom: the British Library' *Australian library journal* February 1974 5–7

2 British Library 'Introducing the British Library' (Free pamphlet to be published in 1975)

3 B Houghton *Out of the dinosaurs: the evolution of the National Lending Library* London, Clive Bingley: Hamden (Conn) Linnet Books, 1974

4 D J Urquhart 'Out of the dinosaurs' NLL review 2 (6) April 1973 183–5

5 J Burkett *Government related library and information services in the United Kingdom* Library Association 3rd rev ed 1974

6 Department of Trade and Industry 'DTI's Statistics and Market Intelligence Library—how it can help you export' *Trade and industry* 28th October 1971 186–8

7 F Cochrane 'Information for exporters: sources and implications for public libraries' *Proceedings of the Public Libraries Conference Blackpool 1971* Library Association 1971 30–40

8 Select committee on public libraries Report 1849

9 J P Lamb *Commercial and technical libraries* Allen and Unwin 1955 19–54

10 C W Black 'Commercial libraries' *International library review* 1970 (2) 485–92

11 Board of Education Public Libraries Committee *Report on public libraries in England and Wales* HMSO 1927 p 128

12 D W Bromley 'Public library commercial services' *Five year's work in librarianship 1961–65* Chapter 17 367–76

13 G Thompson 'The new City Business Library' *Library world* 71 (840) June 1970 367–68

14 A L Smyth *Commercial information: a guide to the commercial library* Manchester Public Library 1969 pp 32

15 A Osborn *and* A L Smyth 'Public use of business and commercial information: a pilot study at the Commercial Library, Manchester Central Library' *Aslib proceedings* 25 (7) July 1973 243–51

16 J Bebbington 'Twenty seven years of co-operation with industry' *Librarian and book world* 49 (2) February 1960 21–6

17 N E Binns 'Co-operative schemes of library service for industry and commerce' *Unesco bulletin for libraries* 15 (6) November–December 1961 310–6

18 G R Stephenson 'Schemes of local co-operation for industry' *Library world* 68 (797) November 1966 126–30

19 H A Chesshyre 'Local co-operation—a positive force' *Aslib proceedings* 18 (4) April 1966 92–107

20 J L Atkins 'Local technical information co-operative schemes' *Aslib proceedings* 19 (11) November 1969 444–53

21 V Whatley 'Commercial data analysis' *RAPRA symposium 1973* Paper 6 p 7

22 J S Widdowson 'Technical help to exporters—the why and how' *Information scientist* 7 (3) September 1973 89–100

23 R S Meyer and G N Rostvold *The library and the economic community: a market analysis of information needs of business and industry in the communities of Pasadena and Pomona* California, 1969

Chapter two

1 S Jast *A note on the commercial library* Manchester Public

Libraries 1919

2 Corporation of Liverpool Free Libraries *Handbook to the Commercial Reference Library* Corporation of Liverpool 1920

3 J P Lamb *Commercial and technical libraries* Allen and Unwin 1955

4 R Vainstein 'Public service to business' *Library journal* 84 (9) 1959 1402–6

5 R S Meyer *and* G N Rostvold *The library and the economic community* Pasadena and Pomona Public Libraries 1969 R M Holt *Focussing library service on the economic community* Del Mar, R M Holt and Associates 1971

6 A Osborn *Report on a pilot study at the Commercial Library, Manchester Central Library, concerning the use and users of publicly available business and commercial information* Aslib Research Department 1973

7 G P Henderson 'Commercial libraries' *Unesco bulletin for libraries* 17 (2) 1963 77–81

8 G Thompson 'The new City Business Library' *Library world* 71 June 1970 367–8

9 Report of the RGS committee on the storage and conservation of maps *Geographical journal* 12 June 1955 182–9

10 G Thompson *Planning and design of library buildings* Architectural Press 1973

11 Z J Shannon 'Public library service to the corporate community' *Special libraries* 65 (1) 1974 12–6

Chapter three

1 Corporation of London *Classification in the City Business Library* City Business Library 1970

2 Department of Trade and Industry *Classification of statistical material in the Statistics and Market Intelligence Library* DTI 1972

3 S Miller *The vertical file and its satellites* Littleton, Libraries Unlimited 1971

4 G Whatmore *News information* London, Crosby Lockwood; Hamden, Conn, Archon 1964

5 K D C Vernon *and* V Lang *The London classification of business studies* London Graduate School of Business Studies 1970

Chapter six

1 I B Beesley 'Statistical publications of the Commission of the

European Communities—a selected bibliography' *Statistical news* No 21 May 1973 21.1–21.7

2 'Recommended basic statistical sources for community use' *Library Association record* November 1968 289–291

Chapter seven

1 F Cochrane 'Information for exporters: sources and implications for public librarians' *Proceedings of the Public Libraries Conference Blackpool 1971* Library Association 1971

2 C A Moser *and* I B Beesley 'United Kingdom official statistics and the European Communities *Journal of the Royal Statistical Society* Series A (General) Vol 136 Part 4 1973 539–582

3 *Government statistical services* Fourth report from the Estimates Committee Session 1966–67 HC 246 HMSO 1966

4 M C Fessey 'The new style Business Monitors' *Trade and Industry* 6th September 1973 503–506

5 A Armstrong 'Industrial library news' *New library world* February 1974 40

Chapter eight

1 M J G Lockyer 'Commodity classifications and codings' *Statistical news* No 24 1974 24.5–24.8

2 M Moran 'Foreign currency exchange problems relating to the book trade' *Library resources and technical services* Vol 17 No 3 Summer 1973 299–307

Chapter nine

1 K D C Vernon *and* V Lang *The London classification of business studies* London Graduate School of Business Studies 1970

2 K D C Vernon *The use of management and business literature* Butterworths 1975

3 K G B Bakewell *How to find out: management and productivity* Pergamon Press 1970

4 H W Johnson *How to use the business library, with sources of business information* South Western Publishing Co, Cincinnati, Ohio 1972

Chapter ten

J Burkett *and* T S Morgan *Special materials in the library* Library Association 1964

D Davinson *The periodicals collection* Andre Deutsch 1969

D Grenfell *Periodicals and serials: their treatment in special libraries* 2nd ed Aslib 1965

Judith A Nientimp *and* Stanley R Greenfield 'The librarian . . . and the subscription agent' *Special libraries* 1972

A D Osborn *Serial publications: their place and treatment in libraries* 2nd revised ed Chicago, American Library Association 1973

Elizabeth B Smith 'Trade literature; its nature, organisation and exploitation' *in* W L Saunders *The provision and use of library and documentation services* Pergamon Press 1966

Chapter twelve

The following are guides to libraries' resources internationally, in the United Kingdom, and in the USA.

International library directory A P Wales Organisation 1971—new edition in preparation

Subject collections in European libraries New York, R R Bowker 1965

World guide to libraries Muenchen-Pullach, Verlag Dokumentation Saur 1970

J Burkett *Government and related library and information services in the United Kingdom* Library Association 3rd rev ed 1974

Ibid Industrial and related library services in the United Kingdom Library Association 1972

Aslib directory 2 vols, Aslib 1968, 1970—new edition in preparation

Directory of London public libraries Association of London Chief Librarians 1973

Economic statistics collections: a directory of research sources in the United Kingdom for business, industry and public affairs Library Association 1970

Guide to government and other libraries and information bureaux Ministry of Defence 1971—new edition to be published by HMSO, expected 1975

Libraries, museums and art galleries yearbook Cambridge, James Clarke and Co Ltd 1971

Library resources in . . . Ten area guides, Library Association 1963

Directories are published of participants in the following regional cooperative schemes:

CADIG—Coventry and District Information Group

CICRIS—West London Cooperative, Industrial and Commercial Reference Information Service

HALDIS—Halifax and District Information Service for Business

HATRICS—Hampshire Technical, Research, Industrial, Commercial Service

NANTIS—Nottingham and Nottinghamshire Technical Information Service

SINTO—Sheffield Interchange Organisation

American library directory New York, R R Bowker 1974

Directory of information resources in the United States: social sciences Washington DC, US Government Printing Office 1973

Directory of special libraries and information centers Detroit, Gale Research 1968

Special libraries directory of Greater New York Special Libraries Association, New York Chapter 1972

Index

Chambers of commerce, 20, 26–8, 153; establishment, 14; overseas, 161; overseas in UK, 155; publications, 132; two nation, 27

Chambre de Commerce et d'Industrie de Paris *Répertoire d'annuaires français*, 78

Chambre Syndicale des Editeurs d'Annuaires, 78

Charges for services, 157, 159, 161

Chartered Insurance Institute, library, 152

Charting the British economy (Marlow), 85

Chatham House Library, 158

Chemical Horizons Inc, publications, 129

Chemical industry (OECD), 94

Chemical industry notes, 87

Chemical market abstracts, 75, 87, 129

Chicago business school, 120

CICRIS, 25

City business courier (CBL), 142

City Business Library, 160; *see also* City of London libraries; *City business courier*, 142; classification of books, 52; classification of directories, 48–50, 67–8; classification of market product data, 50; classification of periodicals, 50; company reports, 75; directories in stock, 76; establishment, 20; history, 22; security system, 68; subject guides, 145

City of London libraries, 35; commercial library established, 19; Commercial Reference Room, 22, 67–8; directory files, 77

City University library *Guide to the library of Lionel Denny House*, 146

Civil Aviation Authority *CAA monthly statistics*, 102

Civil Service Department, Central Management Library, subject guides, 145

Civil service yearbook, 84

Classification, 47–53; of books, 52; of directories, 48–50, 67–8; of management literature, 112–3; of market product and industry data, 50–2; of periodicals, 50

Classifications of commodities, 105; of industries & economic activities, 106–7; of statistics, 105–7

Claude Gill, booklists, 120

Cleveland Commercial Library, 20, 36–7, 161; publications, 145; staff training, 44–5

Clippings *see* cuttings

College libraries, 155–7

Columbia business school, 120

Columbia journal of world business, 124

Commerce international, 132

Commercial attaches, 28, 154–5

Commercial food information (Scientific Indexing & Retrieval service), 88

Commercial libraries *see also* academic libraries, local authority commercial services, government departments, commercial services etc.

Commercial libraries, as departmental libraries, 33–4; history, 13–5; objectives, 31–2; planning, 35–9; present structure, 15–30; special services, 139–40, 146; studies of use, 32

Commercial Reference Room *see* City of London libraries *and* City Business Library

Committee of Librarians and Statisticians, courses, 109; publications, 85

Commodity classifications, 105

Commodity exchanges, establishment, 14

Commodity indexes for the standard international trade classification revised (UN), 105

Commodity prices, 101–2

'Common Customs Tariff', 105–6

Commonwealth, commercial library provision, 161; commercial representatives in UK, 154–5; libraries specialising in, 150, 158

Commonwealth Secretariat, libraries, 150; statistics, 90; surveys, 94

Companies House *see* Companies Registration Office

Companies, overseas, documents required by official register, 74

Companies Registration Office, 69, 73–4, 135, 159

Companies, statutory documents at Companies House, 73

Company annual reports, 75; classification, 53; housing, 38; maintenance of collection, 136; on microfiche, 136, 159; selection and retention policy, 135–6

Company card services *see* card services

Dictating machines for public use, 148
Dictionaries, classification, 53
Dictionaries in management literature, 116
Digest of statistics (Northern Ireland) (HMSO), 97
Digest of Welsh statistics (HMSO), 97
Directories, arrangement and control, 67–9; available free, 66–7; basic stock for business libraries, 66; bibliographies, 77–8; cataloguing, 54; classification, 48–50, 67–8; compilation and publication, 63–5; files, 77; financing of, 64–5; fraudulent, 76; importance of, 63; international, 73; major collections, 76–7; overseas, selection and acquisition, 71–2; selection and acquisition, 65–7; shelving 'pamphlet' materials, 68; suitable shelving for, 37; use for enquiries, 69–71
Director's guide to Europe (Gower Pr), 117
Directory of British associations (CBD), 70, 153
Directory of city connections, 138
Directory of directors, 71
Distribution statistics, 100
Distributive trade statistics: a guide to official sources (HMSO), 84
Doctoral dissertations, European, on microfilm, 119
Dublin commercial library, 35
Dun and Bradstreet credit reporting service, 75

Economic abstracts, 87
Economic activities, classifications of, 106–7
Economic bulletin for Europe (UN), 92
Economic outlook (OECD), 92
Economic quarterly review, 92
Economic reports (Lloyds bank), 27
Economic statistics & economic problems (Nicolson), 85
Economic statistics collections: a directory of research resources in the UK for business, industry and public affairs, 85
Economic titles, 87
Economic trends, 97–8
Economics and general subjects: new publications, 137, 142

Economist, 134; as source for literature reviews, 121
Economist Bookshop, booklists, 120
Economist guide to weights and measures, 104
Economist Intelligence Unit, 121
Education and Science, Department of *Statistics of education*, 102
Edwards, B *Sources of economic and business statistics*, 85
Edwards, Edward, 18
EEC *see* European Economic Community
Electrical Research Association, marketing publications, 108
Electronic industry statistics and their sources, 84
Electronics market abstracts, 87, 129
Elseviers lexicon of international and national units, 104
Embassies, commercial services, 27–9, 154–5
Employment and Productivity, Department of *British labour statistics: historical abstract 1886–1968*, 89; *British labour statistics yearbook*, 102; *Family expenditure survey*, 101
Employment and Productivity, Department of, library, 150
Encyclopaedia of management (Heyel), 116
Energy, Department of, libraries, 148
Energy statistics (EEC), 95
Engineer, 132
Engineering (Reviews of UK statistical sources), 85
Enquiries, points to watch in overseas directories, 72–3; sources for supplementing directory information, 73–6; types that can be answered by directories, 69–71
Enquiry counter, site and layout, 36–7
Environment, Department of, libraries, 151; statistics, 96
Ephemeral material, 47
Esso magazine, 133
Estates gazette, 132
European Association of Directory Publishers, 76
European Atomic Energy Community, statistical publications, 82
European business, 124
European Coal and Steel Community,

statistical publications, 82

European companies (CBD), 69, 73–4, 77

European company information, investigation on business library coverage, 26

European conferences, calendar of (UMIST), 157

European Economic Community, effect on company linkage, 70; London office, 154; obtaining publications from, 108–9; publications, indexing of, 110; statistical publications, 82; statistics, 95; tariff nomenclature, 105–6

European Economic Community: sources of statistics (HMSO), 81–2

European Free Trade Area: sources of statistics (HMSO), 81

European Investment Bank, 109

European official statistical serials on microfiche, 86

Eurostat *see* Statistical Office of the European Communities

Exploitation of stock, 47–8, 139

Export Intelligence Service, 17, 28

Export list (HMSO), 105

Extel company services, 53, 74, 135, 155

Extel company services, cabinets for filing, 38

Family expenditure survey (HMSO), 101

Files, vertical or lateral?, 38

Filing, 40

Financial statistics (HMSO), 102

Financial times, 134–5, 159; commodity prices, 101; FT–SVP business information service, 29–30, 46, 159; A guide to living costs around the world, 101; Guide to FT statistics, 159; indexes covering, 129; information service, 46; library, 29–30, 159; library, company reports at, 135; lists of stockbrokers reports, 137–8; Mirac service, 136, 159; publications, 121; source for literature reviews, 121; source for market research reports, 108; supplements, 138

Financial Times Business Enterprises, 137, 159

Financial times international business yearbook, 116

FIND, 46

Fiscal control, libraries specialising in, 150

Fletcher, J *Use of economics literature*, 81

Food and Agriculture Organisation, *Production yearbook*, 94; statistical publications, 81, 90; *Trade yearbook*, 105

Food statistics: a guide to major official and unofficial UK sources, 84

Foreign . . . *see* overseas . . .

Foreign and Commonwealth Office, 149–50

Foreign statistical documents (Ball), 81

Foreign trade (OECD), 105

Foreign trade: analytical tables (NIMEXE), 95, 106

Foreign trade monthly statistics (EEC), 95

Foreign trade statistics bulletins (OECD), 93

Fortune, 136

France, commercial library provision, 161

France, national statistics, 90

Fraudulent directories, 76

Free materials, directories, 66–7

French embassy, 29

French institute, 155

FT–SVP service, 29–30, 46, 159

Funk and Scott index of corporations and industries, 86, 128

Funk and Scott international index, 75, 86, 128–9

Furniture and fittings, 37–9

Gale Research Company, management publications, 118

GATT: *Compendium of sources: basic commodity statistics*, 81

GATT: *Compendium of sources: international trade statistics*, 81

Gazetteers, classification, 53; selection policy, 138

General Agreement on Tariffs and Trade *see* GATT

General household survey: an introductory report (HMSO), 101

General Register Office *see* Office of Population Censuses and Surveys

General statistics (EEC), 95

General statistics: monthly bulletin (EEC), 82

German embassy, 28

German Federal Republic, Federal Statistical Office: *Survey of German Federal statistics*, 80

German Institute library, 155
Germany, commercial library provision, 161; national statistical office, 109; national statistics, 90
Glasgow commercial library, 19, 22, 35, 160
Goss, Charles W F *London directories 1677–1875*, 78
Government departments, commercial services, 17–8, 148–51
Government publications, overseas, 149–50; collections of, 150
Government Social Survey, 96
Government Statistical Service, 83, 96–7, 107; in relation to EEC, 95
Government statistics, 83–4
Gower Press, publications, 116–7, 119
Greater London Council, statistics, 97
Grocer, 102
Growth of world industry (UN), 94, 104
Guardian, 134
Guide to American directories (Klein), 78
Guide to basic statistics in countries of the ECAFE region (UN), 81
Guide to current official statistics (HMSO), 82
Guide to the classification for overseas trade statistics (HMSO), 98, 106
Guide to foreign trade statistics (US), 80
Guide to FT statistics, 159
Guide to government data: a survey of unpublished social science material in departmental libraries (British Library of Political & Economic Science), 84
Guide to key British enterprises, 69–70
Guide to the library of Lionel Denny House (City University), 146
Guide to the national and provincial directories of England and Wales excluding London, published before 1856 (Norton), 78
Guides, library, 146; subject, 145
Guides to official sources (Interdepartmental Committee on Social and Economic Research), 82–3
Guildhall library *see* City of London libraries *and* City Business Library
Guildstream Research Services, 159

Hamburgisches Welt Wirtschafts-Archiv, 18–9, 161
Hamilton, G E *and* Smart, K I *UK statistics: sources, use and indexing re-*quirements, 110
Handbook for managers (Kluwer-Harrap), 116
Handbook of management (Kempner), 116
Handbook of special librarianship and information work (Aslib), 127
Handbooks to management literature, 116
Handbuch der Grossunternehmen, 72
Harmonised nomenclature for foreign trade statistics of the EEC countries (NIMEXE), 95, 106
Harvard business review, 124
Harvard Graduate School of Business Administration, 24, 120, 122; *see also* Baker Library; bibliographies, 145
Harvey, Joan M *Sources of statistics*, 85, 102
Harvey, Joan M *Statistics Africa*, 80
Harvey, Joan M *Statistics America*, 80
Harvey, Joan M *Statistics Europe*, 80, 82
Haskins and Sells, publications, 137
HATRICS, 25
Health and personal social service statistics (HMSO), 102
Health and Social Security, Department of, libraries, 150–1
Health and social security (Reviews of UK statistical sources), 85
Heinemann, management publications, 120
Henderson, G P *Current British directories*, 70, 77, 116
Her Majesty's Customs and Excise *see* Customs and Excise
Her Majesty's Stationery Office, for acquisition of statistical publications, 108–9; lists, 82, 84
Hertfordshire commercial services, 19
HERTIS, 25
Heyel, Carl *Encyclopaedia of management*, 116
Hints to businessmen, 81
Hispanic and Luso-Brazilian Councils, library, 158
HMSO *see* Her Majesty's Stationery Office
Holborn commercial library, 160
Home Office library, 151
Home Office, statistics, 96
House journals, 133, 151
Household food consumption and expendi-

ture (HMSO), 101

Housing and construction statistics (HMSO), 102

Housing in Great Britain and housing in Northern Ireland (Reviews of UK statistical sources), 85

How to find out about statistics (Burrington), 81

How to find out: management & productivity (Bakewell), 115

How to use the business library, with sources of business information (Johnson), 116

Hull, C *Principal sources of marketing information*, 85

Hull commercial library, 22

HULTIS, 25

IBID (International bibliography, information, documentation), 81

IBM library, 158

ICI library, 158

IMEDE *List of new acquisitions*, 142

Incorporated Society of British Advertisers, 76

Index numbers, 101, 103–4

Index numbers (Crow), 85

Index of industrial production, 83

Index to bibliographies (London Business School), 119

Index to world trade marks (Patent Office), 15

Indexes, management, 124; staff, to business materials, 54–5

Indexing services, 128–9; major titles, 131; on statistics, 85; projects, 110

India, cumulation of annual statistics, 103

Indian High Commission library, 155

Indianapolis commercial library, 20

Industrial Aids Ltd *Published data on European industrial markets*, 81, 85, 108

Industrial fibres (Commonwealth Secretariat), 94

Industrial liaison officers, 24

Industrial Relations Library (MIT) *Library accessions bulletin*, 142

Industrial Society, 121, 158–9

Industrial statistics (EEC), 95

Industrial trends survey (CBI), 153

Industries, classifications of, 106–7

Industry data, classification, 50–2

Industry, Department of *see also* Export Intelligence Service, Small Firms Information Centres, Statistics and Market Intelligence Library, Technical Reports Centre

Industry, Department of *Contents of recent economic journals*, 144; *Economics and general subjects: new publications*, 137; for price statistics, 101; libraries controlled by, 30, 148–9; main library, 17–8, 28, 30; regional offices, 17–8

INFORMA (Information for Minnesota), 45–6

Information files, 48, 53–5

Informations Internationales, 74

Inland Revenue, library, 150; *New books list*, 142; statistics, 96, 102

Input-output tables, 83

Inquiry *see* enquiry

INSEAD (International business school at Fontainbleau), 118, 124

Institute of Bankers, library, 152; subject guides, 145

Institute of Chartered Accountants in England and Wales, library, 152

Institute of Chartered Secretaries, library, 152

Institute of Economic Affairs, 121

Institute of Export, 28

Institute of Marketing, library, 29

Institute of Personnel Management, 118

Institute of Spain, 155

Insurance, history, 14

Inter-American Statistical Institute *Monthly list of publications received*, 80

Inter-departmental Committee on Social & Economic Research *Guides to official sources*, 82–3

Interfile (World Trade Centres), 28

Inter-library cooperation *see* cooperative schemes

International bibliography, information, documentation (Bowker), 81

International Business Report Service Inc, 136

International conversion tables (Naft *and* de Sola), 104

International Cotton Advisory Committee *Cotton-world statistics*, 94

International customs journal, 107

International directories, 73

Newspaper collections, 148
Newspaper indexes, 129
Newspaper libraries, commercial services, 29–30
Newspaper monitoring services *see* press monitoring services
Newspaper press directory, 77
Newspapers, 133–5; cutting, 134, 159; on microfilm, 135; stock at Manchester commercial library, 22; storage and display, 39
Nicolson, R J *Economic statistics and economic problems*, 85
NIMEXE, 95, 106
Nomenclature for customs, trade, etc, 105–6
Nomenclature general des activities economique dans les Communautes europeennes (NACE), 107
Norton, Jane E *Guide to the national and provincial directories of England and Wales, excluding London, published before 1856*, 78
Notices SEF/DAFSA, 74
Nottingham commercial library, 22, 160

Observer, 134
Office for official publications of European Communities *Catalogue of European Community publications 1952–1971*, 82
Office of population censuses and surveys *Census of population*, 83, 96, 100
ORGALIME, 81
Organisation for Economic Cooperation and Development *Catalogue of publications*, 80
Organisation for Economic Co-operation and Development, *Foreign trade*, 105; industry reports, 94; *Main economic indicators*, 91; publications, indexing of, 110; statistical publications, 90
Organisme de Liaison des Industries Metalliques Europeennes *Sources and availability of statistics: a reference manual*, 81
OSTI *see* British Library Research and Development Department
Overseas banks, publications, 132
Overseas, commercial library provision, 161

Overseas commercial representatives in UK, 154–5
Overseas company reports, 136
Overseas Development, Ministry of, library, 150
Overseas development plans at SMIL, 17
Overseas directories, collections of, 76–7; selection and acquisition, 71–2
Overseas directory enquiries, points to watch for, 72–3
Overseas government publications, 149–50
Overseas markets, sources of information, 17, 27
Overseas newspapers, 148
Overseas standards, services from Technical Help to Exporters, 30
Overseas statistics, acquisition, 109
Overseas telephone directories, cataloguing, 53
Overseas trade catalogues at SMIL, 17
Overseas trade statistics of the UK (HMSO), 98
Oxford University Institute of Economics and Statistics, 156; *Bulletin*, 156

Packaged Facts, 46
Pamphlets, classification at Manchester commercial library, 51–2; storage and display, 39, 68
Parmoor, Lord, quotation on objectives of a business library, 31
Patent Office *Index to world trade marks*, 15
Patent Office library *see* Science Reference Library
Patents, 15, 148; deposit collections in public libraries, 20; international, collection at Leeds, 22
Pergamon Press, management publications, 118, 120
Periodical abstracts, major titles, 131
Periodical indexes, major titles, 131
Periodicals, area orientated, major titles, 130–1; arrangement, 133; classification, 50, 133; commodities/products, major titles, 130; cutting, 134; economics/statistics, major titles, 130; finance/investment, major titles, 130; general business, major titles, 129–30; labour/remuneration, major titles, 131; legal,

major titles, 131; management, major titles, 123; marketing/market research, major titles, 131; professional, major titles, 131; selection and retention policies, 127–8; storage and display, 39; trade, 132
Periodicals collection (Davinson), 127
Permanent Consultative Committee on Official Statistics *Guide to current official statistics*, 82
Personal incomes (Reviews of UK statistical sources), 85
Personal social services and voluntary organisations (Reviews of UK statistical sources, 85
Personnel and training abstracts, 124
Philadelphia commercial library, 21
Photocopying equipment, location, 36
PIRA library, 154
PIRA marketing abstracts, 88
Pitman, management publications, 120
Polytechnic libraries, 155–7
Polytechnics, services to industry, 24
Population census (Benjamin), 85
Population censuses, 94
Population statistics *see* demographic statistics
Post office, for obtaining overseas directories, 72
Predicasts, 86–7, 128
Predicasts Corporation, publications, 86–7, 128–9
Prentice-Hall, management publications, 120
Press abstracts, 71
Press cuttings, 159
Press indexes, 71
Press monitoring services, 75–6, 134–5
Price Waterhouse, publications, 137
Prices, 101–2
Prices and Consumer Protection, Department of, libraries, 148
Prices and earnings around the globe (Union Bank of Switzerland), 101
Principal sources of marketing information (Hull), 85
Production statistics, 93–4
Production statistics (UK), 98–100
Production yearbook (FAO), 94
Professional institutions, libraries, 151–2
Profit from facts (HMSO), 83
Public affairs information service bulletin, 87, 128

Public affairs information service foreign language index, 87
Public ledger, 101
Public library commercial services *see* local authority commercial services
Public relations of public libraries, 17
Publications, library, 139–46
Published data on European industrial markets (Industrial Aids Ltd), 81, 85, 108

Quarterly index of manufacturers sales: index of commodities (HMSO), 100

Reading lists, 139, 144–5
Reality of management (Stewart), 113
Recommended basic statistical sources for community use (Committee of Librarians and Statisticians), 85
Redgrave Information Resources Corp *Western European census reports 1960 census period*, 94
Regional statistics, 97
Regional statistics (EEC), 95
Register of Business Names, 74
Registrar of Companies (UK), 73
Registre du Commerce, 74
Repertoire d'annuaires français (Chambre de Commerce et d'Industrie de Paris), 78
Repertoire national des annuaires français, 77–8
Research associations, services, 29, 154
Research index, 75, 88, 128–9
Research Publications Inc, population censuses on microfilm, 94–5
Restricted access services, 157–60
Retail price index, 101; international comparisons, 101
Retail business, 108
Reviews of UK statistical sources (Maunder *rev*), 84
Richtlinien, VDI's, loan service, 18
Road passenger transport (Reviews of UK statistical sources), 85
Robertson, A *and* Johannsen, H *A management glossary*, 116
Rochester (US), commercial library, 20
Rope, Crispin *and* Argenti, John *A new glossary of management techniques*, 116
Rostvold, G N *and* Meyer, R S *The library and the economic community*, 23, 32

Royal Commonwealth Society library, 158
Royal Institute of International Affairs, 158
Royal Statistical Society library, 158
Royal Statistical Society: *Reviews of UK statistical sources*, 84
Rubber and Plastics Research Association, 29
Rylands directory, 69

St Paul public library (US), 45
Sandeau, G *A selective management bibliography*, 118
SASLIC, 25
Science Reference Library, 15, 148
Scientific Instrument Research Association, marketing publications, 108
SCOCLIS (Standing conference of cooperative library information services), 25
Scotland Yard, company fraud squad, 76
Scottish abstract of statistics (HMSO), 97
Security measures against theft, 68–9
Selective management bibliography (Sandeau), 118
Seyd's commercial lists, 74
Sheffield commercial library, 20, 22, 160
Sheffield commercial library *World metal index*, 22–3
Sheffield Interchange Organisation, 25
Sheffield polytechnic, subject guides, 145
Shelf lists, 54
Shelving, 37
Shipping, importance in overseas trade, 14
Shopping areas, tabulations for, 100
SINTO, 25
Small Firms Information Centres, 18, 45, 149
Smart, K I *and* Hamilton, G E *UK statistics: sources, use and indexing requirements*, 110
Social science research and industry (Wilson), 116
Social Science Research Council *Reviews of UK statistical sources*, 84
Social security statistics (HMSO), 83
Social statistics (EEC), 95
Social trends, 97
Societies, commercial services, 29
Society of Motor Manufacturers and Traders *Monthly statistical review*, 94

Sources and availability of statistics: a reference manual (ORGALIME), 81
Sources and nature of the statistics of the UK (Kendall), 84
Sources of economic and business statistics (Edwards), 85
Sources of information (London Business School), 124, 145
Sources of statistics (Harvey), 85, 102
Sources of statistics (Series) (HMSO), 81
South Africa Department of Statistics *Annual report of the Statistical Council and of the Secretary of Statistics*, 80
South Africa House library, 155
Spain, Institute of, 155
Special Libraries Association, 118
Special services of commercial libraries, 139–40, 146
Spezial-Archiv der Deutschen Wirtschaft, 74
Staff, allocation of duties, 41; company libraries, 61–2; deployment, 40; establishment, 40; public use of, 48; qualities, 39–40, 44–5; supervision, 40; training, 19, 42–5
Staff manual, 42–3
Standard and Poor's Corporation, publications, 135
Standard Bank, publications, 132
Standard industrial classification (HMSO), 99, 106–7
Standard international trade classification, 105–6
Standards, loan service by Technical Reports Centre, 18
Standards, overseas, services from Technical Help to Exporters, 30
Standing Conference of Cooperative Library Information Services (SCOCLIS), 25
Stanford, Edward, 138
Stanford Research Institute *Long range planning service*, 108
Statesman's yearbook, 117
Statistical abstract of the United States, 91
Statistical bulletin (International Tin Council), 94
Statistical classification for imported goods and for re-exported goods (HMSO), 105
Statistical news, 82–3
Statistical Office of the European Com-

20; combined with commercial departments, 22
Technical Reports Centre, 18
Telephone directories, overseas, acquisition, 72; selection, 71; cataloguing, 53
Telephone enquiries, overcoming some problems of, 36–7
Telex directories, overseas, acquisition, 72
Texas University, Population Research Center *International population census bibliography*, 81, 95
THE information sheets (Technical Help to Exporters), 30
THE technical digest (Technical Help to Exporters), 30
Theft, preventive measures, 68–9
Thomson Organisation Ltd *Acquisitions*, 142
Times, the, 134; index, 129; supplements, 138
Times 1000, 135–6
Timetables, classification, 53
Top management abstracts, 124
Toronto public library, 161
Town and country planning (Reviews of UK statistical sources), 85
Town guides, 53, 138
Town plans, storage, 38
Trade and industry, 97, 100–1
Trade associations, libraries, 29, 152–3
Trade catalogues, 15, 136, 148; overseas, 17, 149
Trade Census Office, 96
Trade, Department of, *Contents of recent economic journals*, 144; *Economics & general subjects: new publications*, 142; *Hints to businessmen*, 81; libraries, 148; *Overseas trade statistics of the UK*, 98
Trade journals, 132, 148
Trade marks journal, 15
Trade name enquiries, 70
Trade nomenclature, 106
Trade statistics, 92–3, 98
Trade union publications, 151
Translating service, by Technical Help to Exporters, 30; by World Trade Centre, 28
Transport statistics (EEC), 95
Treasury library, 150
Treasury Solicitors Department, library, 150
Tropical Products Institute, library, 150

Typewriters, for public use, 148–9
Ulrich's international periodicals directory, 132
UMIST, library, 157
Unesco statistical yearbook, 91
Unilever information unit, 158
Union Bank of Switzerland *Prices and earnings around the globe*, 101
Union list of statistical serials in British libraries (Committee of Librarians and Statisticians), 85
United Kingdom balance of payments (HMSO), 102
United Kingdom energy statistics (HMSO), 102
UK Government Statistical Service *see* Government Statistical Service
UK Kompass, 69–70, 153
UK, statistics, 90, 96–102; demographic, 100–1; historical development, 96; prices, 101–2; production, 98–100; regional, 97; service and distribution, 100; trade, 98
UK statistics: sources, use and indexing requirements (Hamilton and Smart), 110
United Nations, as publisher of statistics, 89–90; *Bibliography of industrial & distributive trade statistics*, 81; *Demographic yearbook*, 94; *Growth of world industry*, 94, 104; *International standard industrial classification of all economic activities*, 106–7; *Monthly bulletin of statistics*, 91; *National statistical publications issued in 1966*, 81; obtaining publications from, 108; publications, indexing of, 110; *Standard international trade classification*, 105–6; *Statistical yearbook*, 91; *World weights & measures: a handbook for statisticians*, 104; *Yearbook of international trade statistics*, 105
United Nations Economic Commission for Africa *New acquisitions in the UNECA library*, 80
United Nations Economic Commission for Asia and the Far East, as publisher of statistics, 90; *Guide to the basic statistics in countries of the ECAFE region*, 81
United Nations Economic Commission for Europe *Economic bulletin for*

185